Daughter of the King

"The Heart of God"

Enjola Watkins

This book is dedicated to all women and men around the globe. I pray that this book will be very inspirational for you and touch you heart in a way like no other.

Contents

Introduction

"What you should know"

1. Relationship
2. Patience
3. Unconditional Love
4. Endurance
5. Grace
6. Compassion
7. Joy

Introduction

For many years I have always wanted to become an author. I have been writing from the time I was able to pick up a pencil until now. A lot of this was free writing at first, however even though free writing gave me the opportunity for my voice to be heard; I yet and still felt as though there was something greater that I definitely had to write about and publish. Throughout my life I have gone through many challenges just as Angel in this book, and even had to witness others go through life challenges and unimaginable decision making. What makes Angel's story so unique is the fact that she was a Christian. Angel develops a relationship with the Lord at an very early age; just as many of us she decided that she wanted to stray away from the Lord and the church, however because the Lord loved her, He yet and still guided her throughout her journey of life as He does for each and every one of us daily. The Lord smiled upon Angel in her toughest times and even though she rebelled against Him, He did not give up on her He was determined to show her His heart towards her, and many of us. He shows Angel His heart by showing her who He was by the love, the compassion, and Grace that he gives daily. He also showed her that church isn't about what people think of you but it's about Him. Often times a lot people that are not actively in church would look inside the church and say: "I'm not worthy to be a part of a church because those people inside got it all together", or" I'm not living right" and I wouldn't fit in". When the fact of the matter is that, a lot of these challenges, and a lot of those decisions which are made within an individual; whether in church or not; are the same, therefore no one should feel unworthy to be a part of any church, nor want to walk away from the house of the Lord because of what people may think, or what they think of themselves because the Lord has no respecter of persons. We cannot judge ourselves nor can we judge anyone else by their lifestyle or due to their appearance because looks can be deceiving as you will also read in this book. Even though I can relate, this book does not tell my life story, but a story that will help many women, and also men; whether young or old understand how important it is to have a relationship with the Lord, and want to know "The Heart of God".

"The Heart of God"

Chapter One

"Relationship"

Coming into salvation was something that was taught to me ever since I was a little girl. I was eleven years old when I was baptized. The small church in Belle Mede, Kentucky was in full swing. The pastor was preaching, the pianist was playing, the choir was singing, and the whole congregation was praising God. I walked through the aisles to cheers and praise and stood in front of the gathering. I was ready to make Jesus my personal savior. It was Thursday night of our annual summer revival and the house was packed. There were extra chairs placed alongside the pews throughout the aisles and many were holding children in their laps. The roar of the piano and the congregation's singing, clapping, and stomping began to fade as Pastor Davis walked up to me. Pastor Davis's voice was like the calm after a storm, hoarse from preaching, but in full command of everyone's attention.

He asked me, "Do you believe in Jesus?"

I replied boldly, "Yes Sir."

"Do you want to make Him your Lord and savior?"

"Yes Sir."

The whole congregation began to exalt God when Pastor Davis picked me up in his arms and began to cry with a loud voice, "Praise God!"

The following Sunday morning, I stood overlooking a large tub of water at the baptismal. I was draped in cloths that were white as snow: a big white t-shirt and some all-white sweat pants.

Pastor Davis, with open arms, beckoned me, "Come on child."

My heart began to beat extremely fast as I stepped down into the cold tub of water. I could only think to myself, this is it.

Pastor Davis then spoke briefly to the congregation in attendance, and then looked directly at me saying, "Angel Braveheart, I baptize you in the name of Jesus."

He then dipped my body into the cold water. I was made anew, born again, baptized. This event marked the beginning of something brand new that was about to take place in my life.

Later that day as my mom drove us home; my mom looked at me, "Baby I am so proud of you!"

It felt so good to hear my mom tell me this.

"Thank you mommy," I smiled.

As we were pulling into the driveway, I saw my dad and a lot of men moving things out of our house. Mom quickly stopped the car and got out screaming, "John, what's this?"

The only thing I could hear Dad say was, "I'm tired Joanne, I can't do this anymore!"

"But John, we have a daughter!"

Dad took one look at my face pressed against the car window, "That's your daughter!"

Tears began to roll down my eyes. I didn't understand. I could not believe that my dad could literally just say that in my presence.

Mom broke down and got on her knees in tears right in front of him, "Please! What do I have to do John? Please tell me, I'll do anything, please!"

Dad then pushed her aside and started walking towards the car on the driver's side. My mom ran behind him screaming, "No John! Please! I'm begging you; this is our only transportation please! Please!"

He got into the car and looked at me sitting on the passenger side with frustration on his face but with a calm tone, "Angel, get out of the car."

"But dad,"

"Angel!" He got louder, "Get out now!"

So I looked at him trembling with tears in my eyes, "Daddy what's going on? Please daddy, don't...I love you! Please daddy, don't go!"

"Listen to Angel," My mom said while looking at dad through the window of the driver's side of the car, "Don't do this."

Dad became more frustrated with my mom, and the more frustrated he got, the louder he yelled,

"Shut up woman!"

"Angel, get out of the car now! Get out now!"

Dad reached over across me and opened my door. I got out of the car and watched as he spun off followed by the men in the moving truck. I would be a grown woman before I ever saw him again.

Mom was torn. She laid on the bare ground in her lovely yellow dress. Her dark brown hair was hanging over her face. I walked over to her slowly, "It's ok Mom, God is here."

She looked at me with tears in her eyes, "Go into the house Angel, please, just go."

I didn't understand what my mom and dad had previously went through, but I do know that it hurt me to the pit of my heart. My only thought was that Daddy doesn't love us anymore. I slowly walked into the house, emotionally drained to the point that it felt as if I had no physical strength in my body. I went into my room, laid in my bed, and I cried on my pillow for hours.

Then suddenly, a calm and sweet voice said to me, **"Don't cry Angel, I'm here."**

I then jumped up and sat upright in bed looking around wondering where the voice had come from. Fearful but curiously I asked, "Who's there?"

"I AM."

My heart began to race because I could see no one in the room as I looked around feverishly. I felt an indescribable warm presence that was so strong that the hairs on my arms stood in attention. "Who are you?"

"**I am the one that you gave your life to today**,"

I looked up towards the ceiling, "Jesus?"

"**Yes, don't cry. You must know that all things work together for the good of them that love Christ and those who are called according to his purpose.**"

"I don't understand."

He chuckled, "**Angel, one day you will. You must know that it's not your fault your dad left and you must also forgive him for the things he said.**"

"Why should I? He hates us and I hate him!"

"**Angel, you must forgive in order to be forgiven.**"

"How…how do I forgive my dad?"

His voice began to fade, "**I love you Angel, and I will always be here.**"

A few knocks at the door startled me, followed by my mom's voice that seemed full of concern, "Angel?"

"Yes Mom."

She opened the door and walked into the room with a look of bewilderment.

"Who are you talking to?"

"No one"

She sat on my bed and placed her arm around me, "Now, honey, I'm sorry you had to witness what happened with me and your Dad today and I know that this was a very special day for you and how much you wanted to tell your Dad about it." With tears in her eyes she continued, "Listen, I don't care what happens, just know that you will always be my little

Angel and I love you more than anything in the world."

Somberly I said, "I know Mom." She then got up and walked out the room. I also got up and closed the door behind her anxiously. I looked up and whispered, "Jesus, Jesus, Are you there? My mom is gone now." But He didn't respond. I sat on my bed and grabbed my pillow and curled up really tight while saying, "Please come back to me Jesus" and I fell asleep.

The following week was terrible. Mom was late for work every day. Some mornings I even saw her crying. Even though we stayed nearby our relatives, they could only help us with so much. I knew the only person that could change our situation was Jesus. But even when I would go to my room and call for him, I would not get an answer and I did not understand why. It then hit me that it was Saturday and not Sunday. I thought to myself, "Sunday is the Lord's Day" so maybe that is when I will be able to speak with Jesus again. I couldn't wait until Sunday morning.

The next day, my mom and I got ready to go to church and while we were waiting outside on the porch for my auntie to pick us up, I told her that I had to run into the house for just a moment. She affirmed, "Okay, but hurry! You know how Aunt Missy doesn't like to wait… so here is the key, go quickly!"

I ran into the house and went into my room, "Jesus! Jesus, are you there? It's Sunday."

"Honk, Honk!" I heard my Aunt Missy blowing the car horn for me to come out.

I yelled, "I'll be back Jesus!" While running to the car.

When we made it to the church, it was alive. People were clapping and dancing in the presence of God, preparing their hearts for the message that God had laid on Pastor Davis's heart. As soon as Pastor Davis walked in, the whole church stood at attention awaiting the words that he had to say.

"Praise God!" Pastor Davis exclaimed.

"Praise the Lord!" We all said in unity in one voice.

"This is the day that the Lord has made," he continued, "let us rejoice and be glad in it".

While Pastor Davis was speaking, I could only think about Jesus and how his voice was so calming like a warm embrace. I wondered how I could have that incredible feeling all the time.

"Having a relationship with God is very important!" Pastor Davis said sharply and his words got my attention immediately. "All it takes is you as a woman or man of faith to want to have this relationship with him," he exclaimed. He then went on to say, "You already have confessed that He is Lord, you have already given your life to Him, now it's time to have a relationship with the Lord."

Pastor Davis looked throughout the congregation, "We all...when we have a relationship, we all have access to life. But how do we establish this relationship? See, this is the question." Pastor Davis wiped his forehead with a white towel saying, "The first thing is to get to know Jesus through prayer, through worship, and most of all his word."

"A relationship," I whispered.

"Shhh!" Aunt Missy nudged.

After church, we visited my grandmother's. I sat on her porch and thought about what Pastor Davis said. I could hear my Aunt Missy and my grandmother talking in the kitchen. Curiosity beckoned me to get up and stand at the door so that I could hear what they were saying.

"How do you know if you can speak in tongues?" Grandma asked.

"You do not, it's just a gift," Aunt Missy replied, "Do you want the gift Mama?"

"No! I'm not going to mess with that!"

I then walked in, "I do Aunt Missy."

"Angel, you're too young baby. You don't even understand what we are talking about."

I looked at the floor, while curling my fingers around and proceeded, "But isn't that what we as children should do, ask questions to get an understanding?"

"Are you smart mouthing me Angel?"

"No ma'am!"

"Get out and go and play with the other kids and stay out of grown folk business."

I stormed out of the house with tears in my eyes and I ran home. Once I got home, I went straight into my room and began to pace the floor back and forth, and back and forth again.

"God, I want a relationship with you. From this day forth I give you me, all of me. I'm not too young to know that I love you but I need you to help me. Help me understand me and who I am in you so that life can be better for me and my mom. I need you Lord Jesus. Please talk to me."

I then looked up to the heavens, "Lord, I want the gift."

"I heard Pastor Davis say that if I ask that it shall be given; if I seek, I shall find; and that if I knock, the door shall be opened for me."

I immediately thought about what Pastor Davis had said today in his sermon: prayer, worship, and the word. That very night, I sat on my bed and began reading the word of God. I began to pray to God quietly, in a soft whisper.

I heard the voice of the Lord say, "**Stop! Repeat after me.**"

"**Praise the Lord!**"

I repeated, "Praise the Lord!"

"**Thank you Jesus!**"

"Thank you Jesus!"

"Now Angel, I want you to continue saying these things which I have instructed you."

I did as the Lord instructed repetitively and suddenly a blazing fire jolted my body and I began to utter words and sayings of which I knew not the meaning. I didn't quite understand what had taken place, but I did know that it was not like any other experience I had ever had. I felt as though I could fly. Had I had the opportunity to go to heaven in that moment, I would have left that night.

Chapter Two

"Patience"

Years had passed, and my relationship with the Lord was stronger than ever. I heard the Lord more and more and we talked every day. I also noticed a shift taking place in my life. With the process of me growing, I would hear relatives gossip and criticize one another and I knew that those things were not of God, and I despised them. I wanted God to show me more. And the more I wanted, the more He showed me.

"Happy birthday to you! Happy birthday to you!" My mom and my friends sang to me as I sat down at the head of our dining room table. It was now my eighteenth birthday and spending it with my mom and two friends, Remi and Ava, made it priceless.

Remi held the cake nervously. "Okay Angel, Make a wish birthday girl!"

"Okay!" I yelled.

As I began to bend over and blow out the candles, I softly made a wish, "God show me more."

"Yay!" everyone screamed.

"Well ladies I'm going to leave you guys alone." Mom informed us as she left out of the dining room. Remi looked at me and Ava Anxiously.

"Sooo...can we move this gathering in another room?"

"Yeah," I said, "Let's go in my room."

Now Remi and Ava were the only two friends I had in my life. Well, other than Jesus.

I met Remi when all of us church kids would hang out at the roller rink. She was ordering a slice of pizza and I had just so happened to be in the need of a soda. There she was, my best friend, tall, dark-skinned, long hair, round eyes, outgoing and glamorous.

Now Ava, I had known since pre-school and we never lost touch. She's still the same grey-eyed, light- skinned, curly-headed girl.

"Well?" Remi asked with a crafty smile on her face.

"Well…" I said.

"Are you guys excited about starting school next week?"

"Yeah!" Ava and I responded.

"Can you believe that this time next week we will all be college freshmen?" Ava asked.

"Yeah I know," I replied. "That went by so fast. I'm so ready."

"Okay," Ava continued, "I have a question for you guys. Have you guys… you know?"

"You know what?" Remi and I spoke in one voice.

"Had sex?"

Remi immediately jumped up off of the bed and said "Okay I'm not going to lie, I have."

I looked in complete shock, "What?!"

Ava rose up her finger slowly, "Me too."

I looked at them both with my mouth wide open, "With whom? Oh my, gosh you guys! That means you're not virgins anymore."

"Well it looks like you're the only one," Remi stated, "And I know a great candidate for you Angel."

"Who?"

"John Jon,"

"Heck No! No way! That would be a horrible candidate plus I think I'd rather keep my purity."

Remi frowned. "What is that supposed to mean?"

"It means that I don't want to have sex, I want to remain pure."

"Okay Angel, okay, I have had enough!" Remi exclaimed.

"Enough of what?"

"Enough of you acting like miss perfect and holier than thou, like you never thought about sex!"

"I didn't say that Remi."

"So you have?"

"No."

"Oh come on Angel!" She flopped down on the bed. "So let me guess, all you do is talk to God right? I mean really?"

Ava sighed. "Why are you upset Remi? She's just stating her opinion about herself,"

"But she's acting as though she's perfect!"

"Remi, I'm not perfect. I just prefer not to have sex. What's wrong with that?"

"Why?" Remi asked.

"Because of my faith in God and because of the things having sex before marriage could bring."

Remi sat up and folded her arms. "And what is that?"

"Okay… now you're being obnoxious Remi"

"No… Tell me, Angel, because I want to know how someone who is so pure can know what sex would bring if they never had sex."

"Okay Remi, if you really want to do this fine. Sex could bring death spiritually and physically like STDs and uncleanliness."

"So you're saying I'm unclean?"

"No,"

"You asked and I'm just answering your question. And I don't have to have sex to know this. It's in the bible, Roman 6:23: For the wages of sin is death; but the gift of God is eternal life through Jesus Christ our Lord, read it yourself."

"Well…" Remi started laughing, "I guess I'll be dying all the time."

"It's not funny Remi," Ava shunned.

"It is too. I mean really Ava? You're going to sit here and listen to little miss perfect. You can but I'm leaving." Ava quickly grabbed Remi's arm.

"Remi don't leave,"

"Ava, I'm not about to be judged by this wannabe Christian, Saint or whatever?"

I got up from the bed, "Excuse me?"

"You heard me."

Remi got up and stood right in front of me. At this point there was a thickness of tension in the room as we stood there face to face, eye to eye, and chest to chest. "What is your problem with me Remi?"

"My problem is people like you."

"People like me?" I answered, "What gets you so angry about people like me?"

Remi stared at me with fire in her eyes and sweat on her nose, "I hate you people, you so called Bible thumpers…thinking you are perfect!"

Ava became nervous. "Remi Stop it!"

"No Ava she needs to hear this."

My heart began to race. My chest was on fire with anger. I couldn't even swallow. I could not believe my best friend had a problem with my lifestyle. I heard Jesus voice saying, **"Breath Angel do not let her get to you, let her speak."**

She proceeds to say, "Ever since we were little you've been talking about Jesus…how you talk to him… how much he loves you…but have nothing to show for it. Since you're so pure and holy, and you live so perfect then how come you live in this dump…Huh?! I'm not pure nor am I holy but my car and home looks a lot better than yours! Not only that but I have both parents in my life and you only have ONE!"

"Remi stop it!"

"No Ava, let her finish."

"With all pleasure," Remi exclaimed, "Why you don't ask God why I graduated at the top of our class and you didn't Ms. Purity? And while you are at it ask him why am I doing so much better than you?"

Tears rolled down my eyes. I swallowed softly "I didn't know you felt this way about me Remi."

"Well the next time you talk about your purity and quote bible scriptures you should ask your God about all of that! I'm out of here!" She pushed me aside and walked out of the door.

The room was in total silence, Ava then got up from the floor and stood up beside me and grabbed my shoulder "I'm sorry Angel, she didn't mean it."

I wiped the tears from my eyes, "I know."

"Are you going to be okay?"

"Yes, I'm fine."

"Okay, I guess I better get going too." As Ava gathered her things, she turned towards me and smiled, "I love you Angel."

"I love you too Ava," She then walked out the door. I flopped down on my bed and laid back. "Jesus, what just happened?"

"That is not what you really want to ask me. Ask me what you really want to ask me."

I sat up in bed and sighed, "Okay… why do I live the way I live and I serve you? Why do I even strive to be a good person and I don't have anything just as Remi said?"

"Angel, go look into the mirror on your wall."

I got up off of the bed and looked into the mirror.

"Look at what I created. She has everything that she could ever imagine. What she has, money could never buy, nor could it be sold. What do you want Angel?

"I want my mom and me to live in a better home. I want a better car."

"Angel"

"I know…" I interrupted, "Matthew 6:33: But seek ye first the kingdom of God an all his righteousness and all these things shall be added unto you. But I have been seeking God; I have been serving you! Before Remi even asked that I guess I really never thought about it."

"And do you know why?"

"No I don't."

"Because your mind was not on the material things of this world, your mind was on the spiritual things instead. You have been delighting yourself in me and even though you don't have a small sports car like your friend, the car that you do have is working fine and even though you live in a home that you don't like, there has never been a night that rain has poured on your head. You've had joy ever since you were a child and that joy you should never allow to be taken away from you. One day you will have all of the

things you desire. But before you do, there are some things that I want you to do."

"Okay and what are the things I must do?"

"**Well it's not midnight and I do believe that it's still your birthday, so open your mouth.**"

"Huh?"

"**Do you trust me Angel?**"

"Yes, but open my mouth? That's weird?"

He chuckled, "**Open your mouth Angel.**"

I closed my eyes and held my head back and slowly opened my mouth as wide as I could get it. Smoothly a cool breeze circled my mouth and my tasted buds began to feel as though they were dancing on my tongue. "**Now close your mouth and swallow.**"

I did and felt something hit the pit of my stomach. "Wow! What was that?"

"**How do you feel?**"

"Like I brush my teeth and ate dinner."

He laughed, "**Angel I have anointed you to preach the gospel since birth. Now there is an assignment for you. And what I have just given you are the words for this time for my people to hear. I have placed it on the inside of you.**"

"Preach? Oh no, I can't do that. I'm only eighteen and besides who would listen to me? Who would even care to listen to me? And what is Anointed, I mean we have covered a lot of things but we haven't covered that part about me."

"**Angel, we have covered everything, yes only to get you to this point now. You had to go through the process of being groomed just for this and now that your heart is laid with the foundation of me. It is my job to make sure that it does not just end at that foundation but that I build on this foundation a mighty tower and you become a mighty woman in me. You gave me your yes.**"

"I did?"

"**Yes.**"

"When?"

"**When you gave your life to me at the age of eleven, and tonight when you blew out your birthday candles and said show me more.**"

"Yeah, but I didn't think that it would be this." I sat on my bed while scratching my head, "Okay, okay, I just need a minute to take in all of this."

"**That will be fine,**" His voice faded, "**I'll be here.**"

I just sat on my bed shaking my head, "This can't be right...me Anointed, a preacher like Sister Agnew?"

Sister Agnew was the oldest mother and only woman minister at our church. She was very snappy and carried her oil and her bible everywhere she went. If you were out of line, she would come over in her long white dress and her extremely large glasses and pop you and tell you what thus says the Lord.

"Oh my" I gasped, "I don't want to be like Sister Agnew! What have I gotten myself into?"

Later that night I tossed and turned in my bed. I could not sleep. I then began to hear myself preaching over and over and over again. I jumped up, "AHHHhh!! I can't do this! Get out of my head! What is happening to me?" I got on my knees beside the bed, "God I'm sorry I said yes. I didn't know what I was asking. I don't want to know more. I want to be a normal person. I don't want this. Take it back. I'm sorry, please take it away!"

I heard another voice that I didn't recognize, "Angel it's okay."

I jumped back into my bed and threw the covers over my head, "Who are you?"

"I have a message for you,"

"From whom?"

"From Jesus. He said to tell you that if you do not do what he has asked that there will be blood on your hands."

"Blood on my hands?"

"Yes, for there are many souls that could be lost and die an eternal death if you do not complete your assignment."

Tears fell from my eyes as I lifted the covers. I saw a pure white person sitting at the edge of my bed, "Ssshhhhh!!" He placed his finger over his mouth, "I won't harm you." He was so beautiful. I have never seen anything like it. He had long white hair. He was pure white with wings attached to him. He was so bright and light seemed to glow from his skin. He was tall, his arms and legs were long, even his neck was long like a tower. I could only look at him in silent awe. "You must do this Angel; you will be honored in heaven by many."

"But what if I don't want to do it?"

"If you do not complete your assignment, you will perish"

"But that's not fair!"

"That's why you must,"

Within a split second he became so bright that I had to cover my eyes and he was gone. Then suddenly for some reason, extreme exhaustion hit me and I fell asleep.

"C'mon Angel we have to go!" yelled Ava as she was putting the rest of my bags into my car. It was Sunday afternoon, our move-in day at college.

"Alright, I'm coming!" I turned to my mom, "Alright mommy I have to go."

"Oh... Angel, I'm going to miss you so much." With tears in her eyes, she grabbed me, "I love you. Be careful okay?"

"I love you too Mom and I will." I didn't know how to tell my mom what I had experienced the night before. I felt as though she wouldn't understand.

"Angel, let's go!"

I ran towards the car, "I love you Mom! See you soon!" My mom stood at the door waving as we drove off.

"Woohoo!" Ava screamed, "We're free!!!"

I laughed, "Wow Ava, I cannot believe we are in college woohoo!"

"I know girl and you know we are about to have some crazy fun!! Have you talked to Remi?"

"No I haven't talked to her since my birthday dinner."

"Well I think you should talk to her."

"I don't know Ava. I mean I am not mad at her but I don't think that we were actually meant to be friends anyway. Besides we're going to separate schools and I think that it's best for us to just go our separate ways."

"Well, you can't say that I didn't try."

"Yeah, well thanks for trying though"

Ava nudged, "I got you."

We had driven three hours and finally we made it to our destination, Western University. It was filled with so many different people of all races and nationalities. It was like nothing I had ever seen before. People were laughing and walking around and it just seemed so vibrant. Then out of nowhere comes this handsome, tall, dread headed young man. "What's up ladies?"

"Hey," Ava and I replied.

"Let me be the first to welcome you to Western University! My name is Bobby a.k.a. Yung Money."

"I'm Ava and this is my bestie Angel."

"Angel?" Bobby asked, "So was heaven better than earth?"

Ava and I looked at each other and started laughing. "Okay, Yung money is it? I wouldn't know how to answer your question. However, me and my girl Ava have got to find Dream Hall, can you help us locate that dorm please and keep the questions to yourself?"

Bobby laughed, "Alright, alright I can do that."

While walking to our dorm, I noticed a guy outside preaching under a tree to a group of people, "Hey Bobby what are they doing?"

"Oh that's Minister Michael Smoother. He's always having some type of Bible session. I used to go hear him all the time. The boy has a gift. You guys should check him out." A moment later Bobby shouted, "And here we are: Dream Hall the place with all of the women your dreams can hold and my dreams can hold many."

"Well on that note," I said, "Thank you for showing us where Dream Hall was."

"Yeah thank you," Ava concurred.

"Hey can I get a tip for my hard work?"

"Sure," I replied, "Keep all of your comments to yourself." We all laughed.

"Well it was nice meeting you ladies and uh Ava, I'll see you in my dreams." Ava rolled her eyes.

Finally we made it to room 217 of Dream hall. Our room was so huge. We had two beds and a double desk in the middle of the floor. The walls were white and we had a huge bathroom in the back. On the side of each of our beds were closets. It was pretty much empty. The beds were stripped and the room smelled as though it had just been painted with a bucket of fresh paint. The floors were waxed to where you could see your reflection. "Girl I want the bed on the right!" Ava yelled.

"Ava wait! Now before you even run and jump on that bed you better pull out the Lysol and bed covers!"

After Ava and I decorated our room and put everything away, we then decided to stay in and order pizza and have a little girl talk. "So what you think about Bobby?" Ava asked.

"Ava we just got here! Bobby isn't going to be the first nor the last guy you see on this campus."

"I know, but he was so cute and his dreads were so long and his eyes were so big and bright and you know I'm a sucker for some round eyes."

"Yeah, but he is a lot older than you too Ava, so just be careful."

There was suddenly a knock at the door. Ava asked, "Who is it?"

"It's Sheryl, the RA for this floor."

I began to get up from my bed, "okay coming."

I then opened the door and this short little woman wearing some bright red lipstick and a big smile says, "Welcome to Western University ladies. I'm Sheryl Jones your RA Resident Advisor. If there is anything that you need, just feel free to ask."

I shook her hand. "It's nice to meet you Sheryl,"

"Likewise, you must be?"

"Angel and this is Ava."

"Nice to meet you both, I hope you have a wonderful stay here in Dream Hall." Just as Sheryl began to walk away she turned back around towards us, "Oh yeah, I almost forgot, the delivery guy from Pizza Palace is downstairs waiting for you."

"Well why didn't you tell us before making the small talk?"

"Ava!" I nudged.

"What?"

"First," Sheryl interrupted, "I'm sure you are too far away from home to talk to someone you don't know like that. Secondly, I certainly was not going to pay for your pizza and third that was the reason I came up here."

"Ava didn't mean any harm she's just tired from the drive here."

"I'll look over that this time, goodnight ladies," she said as she closed the door.

"Ava! Are you crazy? I mean I would have expected that from Remi but you?"

"I'm hungry she could have at least said that first instead of trying to make a speech."

"Oh my goodness Ava we are hours and many miles away from home. Now I know how grumpy you can get when you're hungry, but please be careful with what you say to people."

"I mean I don't see anything wrong with what I said?"

"Ava!"

"Alright I'll be careful, now let's go get this pizza."

I laughed, "I may have to keep a snack hidden somewhere just for you, wow."

Later that night as I lay down in my bed all I could think about was what the Lord told me. I got up out of my bed and went into our bathroom. I kneeled before the Lord, "Lord I don't know why you would choose me to be a preacher. I just want to go to school and be a regular teen you know and experience this life. I hope you are not upset with me but please just know that I love you and I would do anything for you but that I just can't. I want to have fun and live the normal college life like everyone else. Jesus…do you hear me?" But He didn't respond. I then got up slowly and said with tears in my eyes, "I'm sorry." At that moment, I had literally told the man that I had given my life to that I would not do the one thing that he had asked of me and stepped away from him during that season of my life.

College was so much fun. I met so many new people. Bobby, Ava, and I had become great friends. We did everything together, even though half of the time Ava would spend more time with Bobby than me, but I didn't mind. The work was challenging and everything seemed to be going well. Every now and then I would pray to the Lord, but I didn't really have time to listen. I had to study and hang out with my friends. I remember telling myself that my prayer actually was answered to just be normal (sigh) and it felt great.

"Girl you studying again," Ava said in irritation.

"Yeah I have a test tomorrow."

"But Angel, it's Thursday night and we must go out,"

"No, you can go. I think I'm going to the library later."

"You sure?"

"Yes I'm sure,"

"Okay, well I'm out. I'm meeting Bobby and he said he has something important to talk to me about, whatever that may be."

"Okay be careful."

"I will," she said as she walked out of the door.

I gathered my things and went to the library. After studying so much, I decided to take a break and walk around the library, exploring the book shelf to see if something would catch my eye. On cue, there he was, Minister Michael Smoother. I was so nervous because he was a handsome guy to look upon. My first thought was please don't let him say anything to me. He walked passed me, and I thought to myself, okay great, home free. But on a dime, he stopped and turned around, "Excuse me?"

All I could say to myself was don't say anything stupid, just say yes. "Yes?"

"You were the young lady walking with Bobby on move-in day right?"

I said to myself say yes, "Yes,"

"I thought that was you," he reached out his hand. "My name is Michael."

I said to myself again say yes, as I reached out to shake his hand, "Yes."

He looked at me with a smile and all I could think of was that he is so cute with that perfect smile. "What is your name?" he asked.

I thought, "Okay whatever you do, don't say anything stupid." But what is my name? I looked at him "My name?" Uh too late, that was stupid.

"Yes, you do have one don't you?"

Dear Lord what is my name? Okay calm down, it's just a guy, a nice looking beautiful guy asking for my name, "Yes I do."

"Okay what is it?"

It hit me, I knew my name, "Angel"

"Well nice to meet you Angel."

I slowly exhaled, "Nice to meet you."

"So Angel, what class are you studying for?"

"Chemistry"

"Oh yeah, I've taken that already."

"Really, well maybe you can help me."

"Maybe I can, so this is your first year Angel?"

"Yes it is."

"Yeah, I remember my freshmen year. I was… well that isn't important. Let's just say that when you become a junior you would wish you had the sense you have now that you didn't have then…or is that the other way around?"

"I guess," I replied with a smile. "Well I better go it's getting late and I think I have studied long enough."

"Yeah me too, besides I don't see anything that I would like to read."

I began walking towards the table where my books were as he followed, "Hey Angel, I can't let you walk back to your dorm alone. I mean it was a little bit of daylight outside before you got here but now it's dark."

"I'm okay."

"No, I insist. It won't be a problem at all. Besides I drove here."

"Well I don't know Michael. I don't really know you all that well to be riding with you."

"I promise I won't harm you. You have my word."

"Okay you promise?"

He raised both hands, "You have my word." We walked out to where Michael parked his car and he opened my door. I sat down thinking that I had never been alone with a guy before so I really didn't know what to say or how to spark a conversation. He then got in the car, "Angel!"

"Yeah"

"How old are you Angel… what eighteen?"

"Yes…how old are you?"

"I'm twenty." He cranked up the car, "yeah I remember when I was eighteen."

"You talk as if that was long ago."

"Well, yeah I guess you're right it wasn't that long ago. Do you go to church Angel?"

"Well back home I did,"

"Back home, nah girl, we have to get you back in church here."

"I don't know Michael. I kind of just want to do my own thing now." We pulled up in front of my dorm. "Thank you," I unbuckled my seat belt.

"Anytime Angel"

I turned to get out of the car. "No Angel, allow me." He got out of the car and opened my door, "A woman should never open her own doors when there is a man around."

I stepped out of the car gracefully, "Thank you Michael, it was nice meeting you."

As I turned he grabbed my arm, "I'll be preaching at this church called Grace on Sunday and I would love to see you in the audience on that morning."

"Michael...I don't know, I'll think about it."

"Okay, no pressure, I just hope you make the right decision." I slowly walked away, "Later Angel."

I threw my hand in the air as I walked towards the building. Walking to my room I had the biggest smile on my face. I recapped everything that happened. It felt so good to finally meet a nice guy. But the fact that he was a minister bothered me because I knew that if I was with him, I had to go to church. And at church I would have to talk to the Lord. And the Lord was going talk to me about preaching again and I did not want to go through that.

"What are you smiling about?" Ava asked as I walked through the door.

I flopped down on her bed and leaned up against her, "Girl I think I'm in love."

"Ughh, get off of me! With who?"

"Okay, you remember the guy that was under the tree ministering?"

"No....oh yeah, I do now...the tree preacher."

"Yeah, well he just dropped me off."

"No way! You said you were going to the library to study. This is good for you though cause Angel we have not been to church since we got here and that was three months ago."

"I know and I feel kind of bad too."

"And you should because I have not heard you talk about our Savior in a while and your bible is collecting dust."

"Ava, you don't understand. I kind of just want to do my own thing now you know."

"No, I don't know. Plus I need to go to church after the night I had tonight."

"What happened with Bobby... you said he had something to tell you?"

"Oh girl that was nothing as usual."

"Okay, you know Ava, maybe you're right. This could be a good thing."

"Great! Looks like there will be two more souls sitting under that tree."

I began to lie back in bed, "I guess so."

Lying in my bed that night, I began to think about what Ava said. I had to pray, "Jesus, I'm sorry I haven't talked to you lately but you know how I feel about that whole preaching thing. I mean I'm too young and I just got out on my own. I'll bargain with you. I'll go to church and worship, pray, and serve you if you would just not ask me to preach anymore. I love you Jesus, please think about it."

I shortly fell asleep, but I heard Jesus while I was sleeping, "**Angel I love you too, that bargain you made, made me laugh. I understand that you may fear. However, I**

didn't give you the spirit of fear but of power, love, and a sound mind. There are others that are just like you: chosen to do my will; for many are called but few are chosen." I woke up in a cold sweat and looked up, "You're not giving up are you?"

Sunday came super fast. It was almost as if the Lord had fast forwarded the weekend just to see what my decision would be. Michael would be so excited to know that I was coming to his church. My heart was pounding and I could see my heartbeat through my clothes. "Let's go girl," Ava stated while standing in front of me as I sat on my bed. Then there was a knock at the door. "I bet that's Bobby," she said and opened the door.

"Let's get our praise on y'all," Bobby said while walking in, "Hey I heard this church be packed out too maybe your boy can save a seat for us cause you know it's hot in church as is and I don't want anyone catching the uh, the, Holy Ghost!"

"Boy!" Ava scolds, "My goodness I'm glad you're going,"

"Yeah, yeah, the HG, I'm just saying I saw how them people be falling out and ain't nobody got time for all that."

I laughed and said, "Ok, let's go."

The closer we were to the church, the more I felt nausea trying to come. I was so nervous, not because we were going to church, but because I was about to see Michael in church and I didn't know what to expect. We finally arrived. The parking lot was so far away from the building. It looked as though we would have to walk a mile to get to the building as cars were on every side. "Dang!" Bobby shouted, "I mean my boy doing it like that! I thought we were going to a nice size church not a stadium!"

"Shut up!" Ava said while getting out of the car.

"Looks like I'm going to be a preacher, ain't no telling what the collection plate looking like"

I shook my head, "You will not stop will you."

The building was getting bigger and bigger the closer we walked towards it. Bobby grabbed Ava, "Hey baby wouldn't you love it if I was a preacher?"

"Sure as long as you remember the Holy Ghost and know who he is."

Bobby held up his hands, "Oh so it's like that?"

We walked inside the building. The greeters were so nice while walking in telling us hello and asking us our names. From a distance I saw Michael talking to someone. He noticed me and started to walk towards us with a big smile on his face, "Praise the Lord! You guys came, welcome to Grace. Angel it's so good to see you, how are you?"

"I'm good."

"Okay, who did you bring with you?"

"I'm Ava."

"Okay," Michael shook her hand, while turning towards Bobby. "Oh I know you man, man y'all got Bobby to come inside the church. I know we're in for a good time."

"Why everybody gotta be on me, I serve the Lord." Bobby stated.

"Yeah we know," Michael laughed. "Well go inside, and get comfortable. God's house is your house. Prepare your hearts and let's have church."

"Okay," we all voiced.

He walked off as we entered the sanctuary. The church was something I had never seen before. I thought my church was lively but this church was alive times five. People were in the aisles dancing and shouting, they had big flat screen TVs on the walls and there was not a pulpit with a podium, but a stage with lights and a band. Then all of a sudden a man walked out, "Praise the Lord!"

Bobby whispered, "Wasn't they just praising the Lord?"

"Shhh!" Ava nudged.

"My God, My God!" The man proceeds to say, "God is good I hope you all enjoyed worship because now it is time for the word of God. And today I am so honored to have my son Michael delivering the message on this morning."

"Son?" I complained to myself. His dad is a Pastor, now that's just great. Now I really have to be on my p's and q's. "Lord, this is just getting better and better huh?"

Michael came out after his Dad talked and I was so amazed at how bold he was and how he grasped the people's attention. How he was able to not miss or skip a beat while talking. He broke every scripture down. It was so amazing. I could only think to myself that I can't do that, especially not in front of all those people. I heard the voice of the Lord say, **"Angel, the number of people assigned to your life is greater than these."**

"Okay Lord, please not today, not today,"

"What?" Ava whispered.

"Nothing"

Michael beckoned, "If there be anyone who needs prayer or need a healing or if you just want to turn your life over to Christ, come down to the altar now."

Ava grabbed Bobby's hand and squeezed it tightly. She got up and walked all the way down to the altar without saying anything. I looked at Bobby; Bobby looked at me and said, "I don't know, I guess she wants the HG."

Church was finally over. As we walked out of the doors of the sanctuary, a young guy came and asked "Angel?"

I turned towards him, "Yeah."

He looked relieved, "I was hoping that was you. Michael said to go and get the young lady in the yellow shirt."

I stated to him there are a lot of young ladies with a yellow shirt on."

He laughed, "Right! But there are not a lot of young ladies in a yellow shirt standing with a guy that has his dreads in a Mohawk."

"Hey!" Bobby yelled.

"No harm man, your hair is cool but Michael wants you all to follow me."

We all followed the young man through the crowd of people that were leaving the sanctuary and walked down this long hallway with so many doors.

"Y'all got a Starbucks!!!" Bobby shouted, "What church has a Starbucks and ATMs? Where can I sign up?"

The young man laughed again, "We have a gym too and an arcade."

"In church?" Bobby asked.

"Yeah, but it's for the youth on game night here at the church."

"Now if yawls have a McDonald's it's on!"

The young man couldn't stop laughing at Bobby as he opened the door to a room. "Michael will be here shortly." Ava looked around, "Wow! This room is amazing."

It was a beautiful room. It had caramel colored chairs and a TV mounted on the wall and also a table sitting in the center of the room with chairs. Towards the back were a small office and a restroom. The door opened, "Hey!" Michael greeted as he entered the room, "Did you have a great time?"

"Heck yeah and this church is off the chain!"

Michael then laughed and said, "Well Bobby I'm glad you enjoyed it."

Bobby placed his hand on his cheek, "I have a question…if your folks got all of this, why do you preach under a tree?"

Michael then smiled, "Because I love to preach, it doesn't matter if it's under a tree or on a corner, the word of God is my passion."

"That's awesome," Ava said.

Michael walked over towards me, "Did you enjoy yourself Angel?"

I took a deep swallow because we were standing eye to eye, "Yes I did, and you really brought the word on today."

"God bless you, Angel. Can I talk to you in my office for a second? You guys don't mind do you?"

Ava and Bobby nodded, "No not at all."

Michael and I walked into the office in the back. He grabbed me by the hand while sitting on his desk, "Angel I'm so glad you came today."

"I'm glad I came too Michael."

"I have been thinking about you a lot lately Angel."

"Oh really"

"Yes, I have. It's almost as if I have been looking for you."

My heart began to race as he talked. I cleared my throat, "Looking for me?"

"Yes Angel, I have been searching for a beautiful quiet-spirit woman." He came a little closer, "I only have one question for you. I know it's sudden but I'm only doing what I feel."

"And what's your question?"

"Will you let me be your knight and shining armor?" I chuckled. "What's so funny?" he asked.

"Michael we're in church,"

"Yeah I know but there is nothing wrong with me asking you that question."

I smiled, "I'll give you your answer when the time and setting is right."

"I can respect that. Well I know you have to go. I'll talk to you soon. Here is my card. Feel free to call me anytime because I'm little tired of chasing you at school."

I laughed, "Okay I will."

As Ava, Bobby, and I walked to the car, I could hear him asking me that question over and over again in my head. "Angel, Angel," Ava called, "Girl you okay?"

"Oh she just got hit by cupid that's all," Bobby said.

"Oh please, I'm not hit by cupid."

Ava grabbed my shoulder, "Awe my girls in strong like how cute is that."

I rolled my eyes at Ava, "He's aight I guess."

Bobby took one look at me with his nose up, "Uh huh, yeah we know."

Later that Sunday night I sat in my bathroom because I really needed to talk to Jesus. I got on my knees, "Lord I know that you want me to preach and everything but I really, really don't want to please accept this bargain please. I really like Michael. I think that he's a great guy and everything, but please I just want to get to know him and that's it. I know that he's going to want a woman that is up to his speed, but I'm not ready to be an active Christian again. He's going to want me to pray, fast, and all types of things that I am not ready for nor do I want and the preaching may just scare him away. But thank you so much for understanding and being patient with me all this time. I just can't do it. Amen."

Chapter Three

"Unconditional Love"

Time passed and it was now my junior year at Western University. Life was different. Ava and I moved off campus and into our own place. We even got jobs at a nearby video game rental store. Michael and Bobby had become close. Bobby even turned his life over to the Lord and not for the collection plate thank God. Michael and I were two peas in a pod. We had now been together for two years since I answered his question one night after a revival. I guess the Lord finally put to rest the preaching thing and finally gave me the freedom I wanted. But even though I was free there was yet still a void that needed to be filled on the inside of me. Even though I talked to the Lord and my prayer about the bargain was answered, something was missing.

"There's my girl," Michael's father stated as I walked into their home. "How have you been?"

"I've been good," I replied.

Michael's dad's name was Carl and his mother's name was Kim. They were really nice people that I had grown to love. Michael's dad would always speak into our lives and even tell us a thing or two every now and then. His mother, on the other hand, was very quiet and soft spoken and out of two years of knowing her, she really never had too much to say. However, when she did speak, she spoke whatever was on her mind. "Where is Michael?" I asked him.

"He didn't tell you?"

"Tell me what?"

"He went downtown to pick up a few things, he should be back shortly."

"Okay"

"That guy always sticks you with us huh?"

I smiled. "Always"

"Well make yourself at home. My wife is in the back I'll let her know you're here."

I felt my phone vibrate with a text from Michael saying "I'm on my way babe."

I texted back relieved, "okay."

"Hey Angel," Mrs. Smoother walked out with a big smile.

"Hi Mrs. Smoother, how are you?"

"I'm good and you?"

"I'm fine."

"Where is my son?"

"I have no clue but he texted me that he was on his way."

"Oh okay. So Angel, have a seat, how is school?"

I took a seat, "School is good actually. My grades are good."

"Okay, that's good." After a while of silence I knew she could tell I was getting a little impatient so she asked, "How have my son been treating you?"

I looked at her surprisingly, "He's been great, quite a gentlemen."

"I see you two have been talking for some time now," she continued, "but what I can't understand is why, because you two have nothing in common."

I looked at her with a weird look on my face, "What do you mean?"

"What I'm saying is that he ministers all over and you really don't go to church. He's serving the Lord and you're just living."

Before I could even say anything, I heard the door open and Michael walked in, "Hey!"

I was a bit unnerved on the inside but I kept my composure so that the expression on my face would not show how the inside of me felt. "Hey!" I shouted.

He came over and gave me a hug and sat beside me, "What y'all talking about?"

"Oh I asked your friend why are you two together when you don't have anything in common?"

I thought to myself oh my God, Lord please, this woman will not stop. "We have things in common" Michael informed.

"Like what?"

"Mom really"

"No I want to know."

Michael's dad overhearing the conversation walks in. "What you want to know Honey?"

"I want to know why they are together when then don't have anything in common."

"Well honey you know opposites attract."

She leaned back in her chair, "Yeah okay."

Michael turned towards me, "You ready to go?"

"Wait a minute son; let us talk to you guys for a second."

Michael sighed and sat back down, "Okay Dad what's up?"

"It's been a while since you both have been talking and as parents we would like to ask you two some questions," his dad explained.

Michael nodded, "Okay, what do you two want to know?"

"You want to go first baby?" his dad asked his mom.

"No you can," she replied.

"Alright," his dad looked down and looked up again at Michael and me, "Are you two sexually active?"

I just sat there in complete silence and shock because my mom never asked me that question before. Michael looked at me and looked at his dad and started laughing, "No Dad we're not."

His parents looked at me, "No sir we're not."

"That's good," they both said, "really good."

"You should wait until marriage," his dad continued, "It's better to marry than to burn with passion." His dad then looked at me, "Angel…" I said to myself oh Lord, "Do you love the Lord?"

I then replied, "Yes I do."

"Did you know you are an awesome woman of God Angel and anointed whew! And you've heard it before but not from man until now because you can hear God. You've been hearing him since you were a little girl. Your mom would hear you talking to Him at night and even though she never said anything to you about it she knew you were talking to God. Your family members never could understand why you took so much liking into knowing God and they found it to be strange for a child so young to adore God as much as you did." Tears rolled from my eyes and I slowly bowed my head because everything he said was true. Michael grabbed my hand as his father proceeded to say, "Stop running angel, God has major plans for your life and no matter what happens in this season know that God is with you and he will love you no matter what you do and we love you too."

I lifted up my head, "Thank you."

Michael interrupted and stood up in front of me, "Okay we're going to go somewhere for a little while."

His dad stood up as well, "Okay I love you."

"I love you too Dad, Mom." We then walked out of the house and got into Michael's car, "You're okay babe?"

"Yeah"

Michael laughed, "Daddy got you didn't he? I knew he was going to get you."

"What's so funny about that?"

"No I'm just laughing because people don't expect it and then when he speaks to them, the looks alone on their faces are hilarious. Boo you were crying, awe that touched me."

"Yeah, how does he do that?"

"Well it's called the Prophetic anointing; some of it is discernment as well. He hears from God for people and he tells them what God said."

"Yeah, but how, like how did he know all of those things from my past? And how did he know I could hear God?"

"It's the gift that God has given him. We all have gifts Angel."

"I know that. I just didn't know the types of gifts we could have besides speaking in tongues. I mean I've read the Bible and studied scriptures."

"Really and you never read about spiritual gifts?"

"Well the Bible is a huge book Michael."

"Yeah I know." Michael reached behind his seat and pulls out a small hand Bible, "Okay, 1 Corinthians, chapter twelve, verse four, it says that there are different kinds of gifts, but the same Spirit distributes them. There are different kinds of service, but the same Lord. There are different kinds of working, but in all of them and in everyone it is the same God at work. Now to each one the manifestation of the Spirit is given for the common good. To one there is given through the Spirit a message of wisdom, to another a message of knowledge by means of the same Spirit, to another faith by the same Spirit, to another gifts of healing by that one Spirit, another miraculous powers, to another prophecy, to another distinguishing between spirits, to another speaking in different kinds of tongues, and to still another the interpretation of tongues. All these are the work of one and the same Spirit, and he distributes them to each one, just as he determines."

I took a deep breath, "I don't know how you are going to feel about this Michael, but two years ago God told me that I was anointed to preach his word."

Michael looked at me in shock, "Really two years ago?"

"Yes two years ago."

"Angel that's a long time to keep God waiting, you should be thankful that he has been patient with you for that long."

 "Michael I know, but I told him that I was too young and that I couldn't do that and that I wanted to live my own life. He would show me things and teach me stuff when I was younger up until I turned eighteen. I just had enough. And now I met you and you're serving him and it just makes it even more so complicated for me. I was so happy when I talked to God. I'm still happy but I don't want to have to be a preacher to keep my happiness."

Michael placed his hand on mine, "Angel it's not about being just happy but doing God's will. You're going to go through things yes and let me be the first to tell you that in doing his will, every day will not be a happy day. However, every day will be a life learned lesson taught to you to serve and please Him."

"Michael you don't understand."

"Yes, I do Angel. How do you think I feel? You think I wanted to be a preacher? I ran too, because I just wanted to be a normal kid, but when the Lord has a plan for your life and you made him Lord over your life by accepting and confessing that he is your Savior then He is made sovereign over your life. In symbolic terms, you're the country but he is the government that rules your life and a country with the wrong government cannot stand strong. Yes there will be battles, yes there will be wars, but because of that strong government, My God I feel the Holy Ghost! Nothing can stop nor defeat that country."

"You didn't want to preach?"

"No, I didn't, but I knew that I was brought here for that purpose because just like you he told me too," Michael continued, "Angel I have been through a lot. It's hard being a child of a pastor. It's almost like people expect you to be a preacher or a deacon or something in the church, and I acted out. I wasn't the perfect child. I acted out because I knew I had an assignment but I knew that I didn't want people to think that just because my dad was a preacher I should be a preacher. I didn't want to do what people wanted me to do, I wanted to be myself and know God for myself. So I did my own thing for a while and I got so tired of people saying oh you're going to be a preacher, you're going to be like your daddy. Angel it was tough. If I liked a girl, the whole church knew it. If I bought a beer, the store manager told my dad. If I smoked a cigarette, it was told. I just wanted to be me. The pressure made me run, made me hide, made me want to do me. And had I just did what God wanted me to do at the age of fifteen, I wouldn't have smoked cigarettes, I wouldn't have drunk alcohol, went to strip clubs or clubs and got into trouble with the law, because I would have been under his government. Not saying that I wasn't because through it all he kept me. However, I'm glad because I did find him for myself and I did do what he wanted me to do and not what my mom nor my dad or people but what he wanted me to do. Angel when we are not in place or on our assignment, we hurt others. We leave them in a place that has no air and no life. I was scared too. But because I finally knew the God I served, I shook that off and stepped in place."

"Thank you Michael for sharing your story, but I can't do this."

Michael sighed deeply, "I love you Angel and I'm always praying for you. I just want you to know that you can bypass a whole lot if you do what God says do."

"I think I have bypassed a lot and I didn't have to be a preacher to do that."

Michael shook his head, "Okay," and drove me to my apartment. On the way there, I could tell Michael was a little bothered by the things that I said. He was in complete silence all the way to my apartment and when we got there he didn't even come inside to chill out. He just said that he would talk to me later after he walked me to the door.

"Hey girl," Ava yelled as I walked into the door. "You mean to tell me Mr. Smoother isn't with you tonight?"

Girl, "He just left."

"What's wrong Ms. An-gel?"

"Nothing's wrong A-va,"

"Well girl let me tell you about Bobby crazy self,"

"What happened,"

"Okay we were in the mall and so I decided that I wanted to buy some nice little underwear. You know for him. And he had the nerve to say that I don't need to buy that anymore because were practicing celibacy. I told that Negro that we didn't practice it the night before."

"That's great Ava,"

"For whom... now look everyone is not like you and Michael okay. We have needs."

I laughed, "You're so silly and this is the girl who goes to the altar call every Sunday?"

"Yes, I got to ask for forgiveness."

"So what did Bobby say?"

"Let's just say after I tried them on he changed his mind,"

Oh Ava, "You are wrong for seducing that man when he's trying to live right."

Ava placed her hands on her hips. "What?"

I touched her forehead, "Okay are you sick? Where is my friend who goes to church and actually hears the word?"

"Oh she still here"

"It's like you and Bobby switched places"

"Girl at the end of the day, Bobby knows I'm going to do right, it just may take a little time."

"Yeah okay"

"Okay nothing, you better put a stronger hold on Michael before someone else takes him."

"Girl please, Michael ain't thinking about having sex."

"Yeah right, how do you know?"

"Because I know Ava"

"Mmmmhuh out of two years he haven't touched you once, he might be touching someone else,"

"No, he's not. He doesn't because he respects me and because of our belief."

"Okay"

I rolled my eyes, "Whatever, I'm going to my room. I'm not about to let you poison my mind."

"Okay girl, don't say I didn't warn you."

Weeks passed by and Michael and I really weren't talking as much as we did before. I would call him and he would tell me how busy he was. I would go see him but he was never home. What Ava told me began to sink in. Maybe he had found someone else and wasn't interested in me anymore. So one night Ava and I decide to go to our favorite restaurant called Lakey's. They had the sweetest smelling, most deliciously fluffy, buttery bread rolls. We sat down and got our menus. As soon as I looked over Ava's shoulder, I saw Bobby at the table with a girl. "Ava, where is Bobby?"

"Oh he couldn't make it; he said he had a meeting with the youth ministers at church."

"Oh did he?"

"Yeah"

"Well, um it doesn't look like he's at church to me."

Ava looked at me with her eyes wide open and turned around, "What? Oh I'm about to open up a can of you know what!"

She began to get up. I grabbed her arm, "Ava no!"

"No, let me go!" she said, becoming louder. Everyone in the restaurant began to turn around and I couldn't hold her any longer. She ran over to Bobby's table, "Bobby, who is this?"

I then ran over to the table, "Ava lets go."

"No Angel! Bobby who is this?"

Bobby looking appalled got up from the table, "Man, this my cousin!"

The girl then stood up, "Your cousin?"

All I could do was say, "Oh my God!" Ava, Bobby and the young lady began to argue. The manager of the restaurant then asked us to leave. I grabbed Ava's arm again, "Let's go home Ava now."

The manager affirmed, "If you don't leave I'm calling the police."

Ava was so persistent. "Ava let's go now!" I then pulled her out of the door as she yelled and screamed. Ava was furious the whole ride home. My cell phone ranged, it was Michael. "Hello."

Ava was still yelling and crying. Michael asked, "What's going on?"

"Long story"

"Is she okay?"

"No she's not."

"Where are you?"

"On my way home"

"Can I come see you?"

Even though I hadn't seen him in forever, I looked over at Ava and saw that she was crying really bad, "I'll just call you when I get there."

"Okay Angel talk to you then," we then hung up.

We finally made it home and after I calmed Ava down, she finally fell asleep. I called Michael. "Hey sweetheart," he said.

"Well hello I haven't heard from you."

"I've been so busy babe."

"Yeah I figured that."

"I miss you Angel."

"I miss you too."

"Is Ava okay?"

"Yeah she'll be alright, she's asleep now."

"Can I come over?"

"Michael, you okay? Because it's one in the morning and you've never asked to come see me at this time."

"I know but I really want to see you."

"Okay Michael, come on."

Within minutes later Michael was knocking on the door. I opened the door, "Wow that was fast."

Michael rubbed my cheek, "Well I really wanted to see you,"

We quietly walked to my room and before I could actually get in my room, Michael grabbed me by my waist and kissed me.

"Michael wait, what are you doing?"

He walked further in the room while looking at the floor and looking back up at me, "Angel, I want to make love to you."

I could not believe what he had just said. I had to take a seat on my bed, "Michael, are you serious?"

"Yes, I am Angel, so serious."

"And when did you begin to think about this?"

"I've always thought about this, I love you Angel."

"Okay, but you're a minister and we can't because it's wrong. What about waiting until marriage? What about God?"

Michael kneeled down before me and looked into my eyes, "Angel you're going to be my wife someday anyways. So why not?"

"But what about…"

He placed his hands over my mouth, "Shhhhh. Say no more just relax."

After that night, I didn't even ask myself any questions such as why did I give in? And how could I go back on everything I was taught? And how could he be so strong in faith and a minister of the Gospel and want to lay down with me? And even though I felt these questions trying to come up, I suppressed them with maybe it's not that bad and besides he does love me and he did say I will be his wife someday. After three months of being intimate with Michael, I didn't care anymore. It was almost as if it was normal for us. I became so numb and he as well that we didn't even care to discuss it. And because we didn't discuss it, our lives took a turn for the worse.

"Angel, Angel," Ava said while nudging me to wake up in the break room at work. "Are you okay?"

"Yeah I'm fine."

"You better be glad Mr. Walter didn't come in and catch you sleeping. You stayed up late last night?"

I rubbed my face, "No Ava I'm just tired,"

"Angel you been sleeping like crazy and your attitude has changed."

"Well when you go to school and work and have a man it does tire you out."

"Tell me about it, maybe you need some vitamins; I would say you're pregnant but we know that's not possible because you and Michael not getting down like that."

I looked at her with a smirk on my face and changed the subject, "What time you get off?"

I just couldn't tell Ava about Michael and I because I knew she would throw it in my face. Besides, I didn't want to hear anything she had to say. Ava answered, "I get off in five, four, three, two, and one, see ya! 6 o'clock I'm out. Okay girl I'll see you in an hour,"

"Yeah alright." I took a moment and thought about what Ava said about pregnancy. I shook my head, no way.

I could not wait until 7 o'clock. It's like time was going by so slow. No one was coming in the store so I decided to take a nap. "Angel!" I jumped up in fright. It was Mr. Walter standing right in front of me with his tall, dark eyes and shiny bald head. "Do you know what time it is girl?"

I looked at him in total shock and looked at the clock on the wall, "12 a.m. I'm so sorry."

He was so angry it was almost as if I could hear him roar as he spoke. "I am so disappointed in you Angel. What if someone came in and took everything? Not only did you put my store in danger of being robbed but you put yourself in danger!"

I heard a knock on the door and I turned around and it was Michael. I put my head down and whispered, "This is so embarrassing."

Mr. Walter pointed at me while walking to the door, "I'm not done with you yet."

"Hello sir," Michael ran in. "Angel, are you okay? I have been calling and calling." He took a closer look at me, "Angel, did you just wake up?"

Mr. Walter yelled, "Angel we'll discuss this tomorrow followed by some paperwork."

"What is he talking about Angel?"

I looked sadly at Mr. Walter, "Yes sir I understand" and turned towards Michael, "Can we go please?"

Michael followed me home. When we both got out of our cars, Michael came around my car and stood in front of me. "Tell me you did not fall asleep at work babe."

"I didn't fall asleep at work babe."

"Angel it's not funny," we walked into the apartment.

"I'm not being funny. I'm just saying what you said to tell you."

"Angel, what is wrong with you?"

"Michael, please... all I want to do is take a shower and go to bed!"

"Go to bed? Angel, You just woke up!"

A rage of anger overcame me, "Michael go home!" I quickly walked to my room and slammed the door. I soon heard the front door close and for some reason I didn't care. It was as if I didn't have any feeling or thought about anything I had just done.

The next day after hearing Mr. Walter's long lecture and getting a write up for sleeping at work, I realized what I had done to Michael was mean so I decided to give him a call after the meeting with Mr. Walter. I told him that I was sorry and had just had a bad day and that things had gotten a little stressful for me lately. Michael said that he understood, we said our love yous and hung up the phone.

Later that day when I arrived home, I noticed that Ava was walking out of my room. "Ava, are you looking for something."

"Oh yeah I was just looking for some tampons."

"Don't you think you should have asked first?"

"Yeah I should have but you don't have any anyways so I don't have to."

I looked at her in frustration, "Well next time ask please."

She smiled, "Sure thing!"

I thought to myself while walking in my room, "I do have some in here." I walked to my bathroom and looked under my sink, "I really don't have any." I sat on my bed in deep thought, "I don't even remember buying any for the past months. Okay this can't be right." I grabbed my calendar off my wall and noticed that none of my cycle dates were marked. My heart began to race while looking at the calendar knowing that this could only mean one or two things: either I had a female problem or I was pregnant. I needed to ask someone about this that knew and the only person that I could talk to at this time was Ava and I dread talking to her but I had to. "Ava!"

"Yeah!" she yelled back.

"Come here for a second please!"

She walked to my room door, "Wasup?"

"I need to ask you something."

She then walked in my room, "What?"

I had to think of something fast; because I could not tell her I had been having sex with Michael for the past three months.

"What girl, you're scaring me."

"Never mind," I just couldn't think of anything without her knowing what was going on with me.

"Okay," she walked back out the room.

I could not believe that I could possibly be pregnant. Michael and I were always careful even though we didn't use condoms so I knew that this had to be wrong. I thought about going to see a doctor because maybe I was having a female problem because I couldn't possibly be pregnant.

The next day I decided to go to a nearby clinic. They took some fluids, ran some tests, and told me to lie down and rest in the bed in one of the rooms. The only thing that I could say while waiting on the doctor was "Lord please don't let me be pregnant, Lord please don't let me be pregnant."

"Hello," the doctor said while walking in with a clip board in his hand.

"Hello."

"Angel is it?" He walked to the other side of the room, sat down on a small rolling stool, and rolled over towards me, "Congratulations Angel you're pregnant."

I didn't quite hear him because it's almost as if when he said the word pregnant I lost my hearing for a split second. I sighed, "Okay so there is nothing wrong with me right?"

"No nothing is wrong you're just pregnant."

I then looked at him, "Are you serious?"

He smiled, "Very serious." He got up from his stool. "My nurse will be with you shortly so that we can get you set up on your next appointment and once again congratulations." He walked out of the door.

I just sat there on the bed in silence. The nurse came in and told me everything I needed to know and I left. I didn't feel like calling Michael and I certainly didn't feel like talking to Ava. When I got home I had thrown everything the nurse gave me in the dumpster near our apartment. "There she is," Bobby yelled as I walked in the apartment. I didn't even respond back, "What's wrong Angel?"

I then straighten up my face and said, "Nothing Bobby I'm good, what y'all watching?"

"Oh just some movie Ava got us watching,"

"And it's a good movie," Ava interrupted.

Bobby murmured, "Yeah good and boring."

"Well I'm going to my room, enjoy the movie guys." I walked into my room, closed the door, and laid in my bed and cried. I kept thinking how could I be so stupid and how this would affect my life and what would my mom say and my family and how disappointed some would be and how happy others would be because of how I was labeled as little miss goody two shoes.

"Knock, knock"

I jumped up and wiped the tears from my eyes, "Who is it?"

"It's Michael."

"Come in."

He walked in with a big smile on his face shouting, "Angel you would not believe the day I had today. It was amazing! God is off the chain!"

"What happened?"

"You are now looking at the Youth Pastor of Grace International Church. I got a salary and everything!"

"Oh that's wonderful Michael. I'm so happy for you. So your dad finally gave you the position."

He exhaled and said, "Finally, I knew he was adamant about me not being a pastor there at first because he's my dad, but he couldn't stop it. God had to break him down!"

I just couldn't tell Michael that he was about to be a dad. He was so happy and going on and on about the ideas God had given him about the youth ministry. "How was your day Angel?"

"It was good."

"You've been sleeping? Your eyes are a little red."

"You can say that."

"Okay babe you have gots to stop sleeping so much. I'm starting to think you're pregnant and that would not be good at all."

I took a deep swallow, "No it wouldn't." I laughed it off as my heart sunk in my chest. I could not believe this was happening to me. It took everything in me to hold all of my tears back while Michael was talking.

"Put on your best dress. Fix up and look nice. I will be back to take my lady somewhere special so that we can celebrate what God is doing in our lives."

I really didn't want to go feeling the way that I felt but seeing how happy he was I didn't want to spoil his moment of happiness. Besides he did say that it would not be good.

As Michael and I sat at the table of the restaurant, we continued to talk about the ministry and things that happened that week. The aroma of the different foods in the restaurant made me nauseated. I tried to swallow but my eyes would water. "Excuse me," I jumped up and grabbed my purse.

Michael looked concerned, "What's wrong?"

I held up my hand as if to say it would just be a moment and ran into the restroom.

After I threw up, I sat on the floor of the bathroom stall and cried so hard. "God why is this happening to me?!"

A young lady then knocked on the door of the stall and asked, "Are you okay?"

"No, I'm not!"

She then asked politely, "Do you want me to go and get someone for you?"

I got up off of the floor and opened the door of the stall and told her, "No thank you. I'm fine, thanks for asking."

"No problem, everything will be ok." She walked out of the bathroom.

I had to fix my face because I didn't want Michael to notice I had been crying in the restroom. After I fixed my face, I took a deep breath and put a smile on my face and walked back to our table and noticed that the food had arrived.

Michael looked up at me smiling, "I thought I was going to have to come get you."

I laughed, "No."

"What were you doing?"

"Oh I had to tell Ava to unplug the iron. I forgot about it, and to use the little girls' room."

He just looked at me and smiled.

Days past by since the night Michael and I went out. I was only eight weeks but I looked bigger. I was getting sicker and sicker. And the sicker I got, the more I didn't want anyone to see me. Yet the more Michael wanted us to go see people and go to events together. I couldn't keep this to myself any longer. I had to tell someone, but whom?

I went to Michaels home to see him off before he left to go and preach overseas. He was so excited about going to Europe and I was so happy for him. "Awe sweetheart," I said as he was packing, "I'm not going to see you for two whole weeks."

"Yeah I'm going to miss you," he held me close to him. "And you better be good while I'm gone,"

"Oh I will be Mr. Smoother."

"You know Angel, something has changed about you."

"What do you mean?"

"I don't know but it's something."

"Yeah right"

"No I'm serious. You talking to someone else?"

"Really Michael?"

"I just asked. I just get a funny feeling whenever we're together but it may just be me."

"You always have funny feelings"

He laughed, "Yeah I guess you're right."

"Alright," his mom said as she walked in the room, "It's time to go to the airport, don't want you to miss your flight."

Michael gathered his things, "Yeah we better hit the road Mom,"

We all left for the airport. When we arrived at the airport, the thought of there was someone growing inside of me was starting to eat away at me. They had no idea what so ever. We walked Michael to the terminal. He hugged his mom and told her he loved her. Then he walked up to me and grabbed my hand, "I'm going to miss you too Angel and I love you so much. Pray for me okay and I will call you as soon as I get there."

"I will and I love you too Michael."

"Mom, take care of my girl."

"Boy please, she will be alright!" She walked towards me as Michael walked away, "Well Angel, looks like it's us girls for this weekend."

"Yeah it looks that way."

We got into the car and drove to their home. As we walked through the door I suddenly couldn't take it anymore, "Mrs. Smoother, I need to talk to you about something."

"Well Angel, let's go into the room and have a girl one on one." We walked into the den. "You want something to drink Angel?"

"No thank you I'm good."

"Is something wrong?"

"Well it depends on how you look at it."

"Okay, what is it?"

"Remember how you and Pastor Smoother sat me and Michael down and asked us about sex?"

"Yeah that was a while back though, you want to ask questions about sex?"

"No."

"Okay, so what was it?"

I took a deep breath, "Well I know that when you have sex..."

She interrupted, "Girl, cut the small talk, what's going on?"

"I'm pregnant." The room became silent and the expression on her face alone burned a hole in me.

"By who Angel?"

I became nervous, "Michael."

"I thought y'all weren't having sex."

"We weren't but one thing lead to another and we started and now I'm pregnant."

"Lord, have mercy, Angel!"

"I know." Tears began to roll down my face.

"How far along are you?"

"Eight weeks I think?"

"Have you been to the doctor?"

"Yes I have,"

"Michael doesn't know, does he?"

"No."

"And you've been keeping this from him?"

"I was going to tell him eventually."

"When?" she replied sarcastically, "When you give birth?"

"Well I don't think I'm going to go through with it."

"What do you mean Angel?"

"I want to have an abortion."

She sat down while looking at the floor and looked up at me, "Well it's your decision and there are a lot of abortion clinics. There's actually one on Hillmans Road."

I looked at her and looked down, "I know."

She then said, "But before you go I think you should at least tell Michael."

"I will."

"When he calls Angel tell him."

"Okay I will."

I felt so much better that someone knew what was going on with me but I still did not want to tell Michael, especially while he was away doing God's work. I then left and went home.

While lying in my bed, I thought about how I just told my boyfriend's mother that I was pregnant and how she didn't flip and even told me about an abortion clinic. "Lord I know it's been a while since we have talked but I need you to help me with this one please, I can't have a baby right now. I know that people think abortions are wrong but I've also heard that it wasn't as long as it's the first trimester, but I need to know what you think. If you don't want me to have an abortion, give me a sign. Lord, please talk to me."

My phone rang. It was Michael, "Hey Baby, how are you?"

"I'm good and that was fast."

"No I haven't made it yet. The second flight got delayed for a couple of hours." I could hear Mrs. Smoothers voice telling me to tell him in my head but I just couldn't. We talked until he had to board the plane.

The next day Michael's Mom called me and the first thing she asked was, "Did you tell him?"

"No, I couldn't because he has been so excited and I didn't want him to have to think about that while he was over there."

"Well yeah but as soon as he gets back tell him because if you don't I will."

"Okay I will."

The days began to go by so fast and I still did not here from God. I knew then that I was so far away from him that I couldn't even hear him anymore. At night I would find myself pleading to God and giving him all of the reasons that I thought would be legitimate reasons to have an abortion. I cried, and cried and pleaded because I didn't understand and I knew that He would tell me, but He did not respond. I became angry with the Lord, "I guess you want me to do this then because you're not saying anything to me! Can't you see I need your help?" The more I cried, the angrier I became, yet He did not respond.

Michael had finally arrived home and asked me if I could come and see him. I told him I would and came right over. We sat in his room as he told me how beautiful Europe was and how services were there. I looked into his eyes and touched his face, "That's wonderful babe but I have something to tell you."

Michael looked concerned, "What is it Angel?"

A knot came up in my stomach and I began to start sweating. I sat up in the bed beside him, "Michael I'm pregnant."

He then looked at me with his tight brown eyes, "I know."

It took me by surprise. "How did you know? Your mom told you didn't she?"

"No you told my mom?"

(sigh) "I feel so much better."

"Why would you tell my mom?"

"I had no one else to talk to."

He looked at me as though he was angry, "You had me."

"Well does it matter now?"

Michael stood up, "Yes it matters because now I have to hear her mouth, Dad's mouth, and you know my mom likes telling my business."

"Well I'm sorry. I didn't know what to do."

"It's cool, I'm tripping. I'm sorry."

"Wait a minute, how did you know I was pregnant?"

"Angel, I have been with you long enough to know everything about you. I know how your mind works and how your body changes. I pretty much have studied everything about you, so that's how I knew."

I grabbed his hand as he was standing, "but I'm not going through with it."

He pulled away from me, "What do you mean you're not going through with it?"

"I talked to your mom and told her I was going to have an abortion."

"What?! Oh no Angel, no I can't let you do this!"

"But Michael we're too young, a baby is a lot and besides what about your ministry?"

"Angel, family is ministry. Please, please don't do that."

I began to cry, "But I have no choice."

"Yes you do, marry me!"

"I can't where too young."

Michael's voice became louder, "God! Angel! Are you serious?! You're willing to kill a child because you're too young?"

"You don't understand. How could we take care of a baby now?"

"With God we can do all things, where is your faith Angel?"

"I don't know, but I do know that we cannot have a baby right now." I placed my hands over my face in shame, guilt, and agony.

Michael kneeled down before me with tears in his eyes, "Baby look at me please." As he grabbed my hands from my face, "Please don't kill my child."

"But it's not a child Michael."

"What about God baby?"

"I have prayed to God. He doesn't care. He hasn't responded."

"Well marry me."

I looked at him with tears in my eyes, "I'm sorry but I can't."

Michael became so angry that he knocked over everything he could touch. His parents ran into the room. "Angel, are you okay?" Mr. Smoother asked.

"Yeah I'm fine."

Michael walked over to me with anger on his face and tears in his eyes, "If you do that I will never love you again nor will I forgive you and I mean it!" "I'm out of here!" He stormed out of the room.

Michael's dad slowly walked over and touched my shoulder, "No matter what Angel, I still love you."

I wiped my eyes, got up from the bed and ran out of the door. When I got into my car it felt as though I couldn't breathe. I finally gasped and screamed with a loud voice letting out all of the shame, all of the guilt, all of the pain. I could not find the words to say, the only thing I could do was scream. I laid my head on the stirring wheel of my car. I tried to calm myself down. I asked, "God why? Why me? Why this? Please give me the answer please help me." Again, He did not respond. I cranked up my car, and drove home.

The next day I had decided to go on with the abortion, and even though I was supposed to bring someone with me, I just had to go alone. My phone rang while I was getting ready to go. It was Michael's mother. I answered, "Hello."

"Hey Angel,"

"Hi Mrs. Smoother,"

"What are you doing?"

"I'm getting ready to go."

"Go where?"

"Please don't make me say it."

"You have money?"

I looked at my phone like really? "Yeah I do...well I have to go now."

"Okay Angel bye."

I hung up the phone, "Okay God, last chance. If you don't want me to go through with this let something happen and that way I won't go." Again, there was no reply. Therefore, I grabbed my keys and my purse and I left.

When I arrived at the abortion clinic there were so many people standing outside with picket signs in protest. There were people holding Bibles in their hands yelling, "You will burn in hell! God will deny you! What if you were aborted?" A lady holding a Bible then ran up to me, "Sister you don't want to do this, let's go to the church and talk about it."

I became frightened and out of nowhere another lady with long hair and brown eyes said, "There you are." She grabbed me by the arm, "she's going in to get a friend."

The lady with the bible looked at her and me, "Oh okay, bring her out of that wicked place!"

The lady that grabbed my arm replied, "Will do."

There was a police officer at the door and he spoke to the lady that ushered me in, "Hey Doris!" He said.

"Hey!"

He continued, "They're a little hostile today."

She laughed, "Yeah every day." She looked at me, "You have your ID baby?"

"Yeah I do." I reached in my bag and pulled out my wallet and showed it to the police officer.

He looked at it, "Go in."

Doris grabbed my hand, "Come on baby."

As I slowly walked up the steps I could feel death. It was deeply void. It was if a part of me had left my body the closer and closer we got to the sitting area. When we arrived, Doris asked, "What's your name baby?"

"Um, Angel."

She walked around this bullet proof window and asked, "Braveheart?"

I replied, "Yeah."

She nodded, "Okay wait right there a nurse will be with you."

As I sat there I noticed that there weren't a lot of people in the waiting area. It looked dreary and it was so cold in the building. I thought to myself, "Angel be strong you can do this." I looked at my phone to see if Michael or anybody called because I thought that if someone called that it would be my sign. However, no one called. I said to myself, "Okay I guess this is it."

"Angel?" I heard the nurse say my name. I got up and she looked at me with a smile. She handed me a clipboard with some papers on it and a pen, "I want you to fill out this and pay

Doris. And when you're done," she pointed, "push that button on the door and they'll let you in the back."

"Okay." I replied.

After I finished the paperwork, I took it to Doris and paid her. I pressed the button just as the nurse instructed and Doris buzzed back from the office, "Okay baby go in."

I walked in this room filled with hundreds of women. Some were yelling and cursing on their phones. Others were crying and there were some that were laughing and talking to each other. A nurse came and stood beside me, "Find a seat. We will be with you shortly."

I looked at the crowd of women and saw an empty seat. I sat down and exhaled because I thought I would be the only one there that day but to my surprise it was a lot of women who were there. I sat as we were called in groups of ten. Finally my name was called and the ten of us went to a small room where a lady named

Rebecca talked to us about abortions. She explained that it's a normal thing to go through and that we all have many things that we must go through and not to let the people outside make us feel bad because they don't understand what we go through at home. We then moved to another room where we had to be checked for STDs, HIV, and AIDS. Next, we had to have a sonogram. As I walked into the sonogram room there was a nurse sitting at a desk. "Hello," she greeted.

I nodded, "Hi."

She handed me a gown, and said, "Go behind that curtain and take off your pants and undies. Put on this gown and come lay down on the table for me." I did as she instructed. "Open your legs." I took a deep breath and did as she instructed again. "Ah there it goes. You wanna see it?"

Abruptly I replied, "No."

"Okay well I'm all done. You can get dressed now."

I walked out and saw the other nine ladies that were ahead of me standing in a hallway. Another nurse came and stood in front of us, "Okay ladies, go up to the third floor and have a seat."

We all walked up the stairs one behind the other. When we got up to the third floor, another nurse greeted us with a tray of medicine in a cup. She told the ladies up ahead to grab one and take it and get some water from the fountain. She then directed us to go into a waiting room and told us that we would each be called in a little bit. As the ladies and I sat there, one of them asked, "Whose first time is it?" I slowly picked my hand up. She smiled, "Oh okay then."

I asked, "I'm the only one?"

Then the lady looked around, "Apparently so."

One girl broke the silence, "This is my second."

Another said that it was her fourth and another, her sixth and so on. The lady that initially asked the question nodded, "Well this is my tenth." I gasped as she proceeded, "Girl please I don't have time for no kids."

They all began to share their reasons with us. One said that it's because she is homeless and another girl asked her, "Well how you pay for this?"

While laughing the girl stated, "I stole stuff and exchanged it for money. I ain't going to lie about it. I had to do what I had to do."

Another young lady explained, "Well my boyfriend made me come it was either that or giving up everything I had at home with him."

One lady with red hair and blue eyes interrupted, "Well I just can't raise twins on my own."

I looked at her in shock, "You're pregnant with twins?!"

"Yeah and this is the second time, I already have four at home that I can barely raise by myself."

The nurse called my name. "Alright baby girl," one of the women said. "Don't feel bad just get it over with."

The pill they had given me earlier made me feel a little strange. Everything began to slow down and I felt so relaxed. I followed the nurse into a small room with a table. The nurse opened the door. "Okay I'm Lydia and I will be your coach."

My eyes became wider, "coach? Is this going to hurt?"

She picked up a gown and a blanket behind her, "well… yeah just a little bit."

"Have you ever done this before Lydia?"

She then looked at me, "Yeah I have."

I went behind the curtain and got dressed and laid on the table. She rolled out the foot holders at the end of the table and another short old nurse came in from behind a curtain rolling a table filled with sharp knives and tubes. "Hey Lydia," she said, "I thought you had left us."

Lydia then smiled at the woman, "No, I just got back in from out of town today and came in."

The old lady looked at me, "What's your name?"

"Angel."

She laughed, "Oh okay, you wasn't no Angel when you got that baby." Lydia looked at me because I had a weird expression on my face, "Don't pay any attention to her."

"Oh she better," the lady affirmed, "because this is about to hurt." The old nurse walked up to my side of the table, "But it would hurt even more had you given birth."

Lydia rolled her eyes. "Do your job woman."

The doctor came in. He had dark hair, dark eyes. He didn't greet anyone, nor crack a smile. He just methodically sat down on a chair as the little short old lady put the utensils in place. He finally spoke, "Hold your legs up straight and take a deep breath." I couldn't see what he was doing because of the blanket. He continued, "Okay you're going to feel this in a little bit."

I began to scream and Lydia grabbed my hand, "Shhhh it's okay I'm here."

"But it hurts." I cried.

"I know just look at me Angel and breath."

"No it hurts please hurry up." The pain got worse and worse and I screamed again.

The doctor looked up at me, "Listen, if you don't relax, I could mess up something. So listen to Lydia and relax. I'm almost done."

Lydia coached, "Breathe." I breathed. "Now Angel let's count to twenty." I counted slowly with her and I suddenly felt the life leave my body. It was a feeling I had never felt before. The doctor immediately left out of the room. I put my head back and thought to myself, "What have I done?"

The short old nurse began to clean up and gave me some towels, "I told you it was going to hurt."

"Stop it old woman," Lydia urged her.

The short old lady looked at me, "I'm sorry baby. I bet you think I'm crazy. I was only telling you the truth. But I will tell you this, before you leave here, repent and walk away and don't think about it anymore."

I got dressed and walked out of the door behind Lydia. Lydia looked at me and asked, "You're okay?"

"Yeah I'm fine."

"Okay Angel sit here for a moment and I'll be back to check on you."

I sat there for half an hour until she came back. She instructed me to get rest and that my body will get back to normal within weeks. As I walked out of that building I didn't see the mob anymore. I thought to myself, "Was that the sign that God was giving me? Because now they're all gone?" I got in my car and went home. When I arrived home, the house was in total silence. I figured Ava was with Bobby and I still didn't get a phone call from Michael. My phone finally rang ending the silence. I saw that it was Michael's mom. I answered, "Hey Angel, did you do it?"

"Yes I did but I need to get some rest. I had a long day."

"Okay, okay, you get some rest."

I laid down and fell asleep. Suddenly the sound of someone whimpering woke me up. I saw that my bathroom light was on so I got up and slowly walked to the bathroom and behold there was a tall black man standing in my bathtub. The whimpering I heard was a baby that he held in his hands, He was so dark that I couldn't see his face. I couldn't believe my eyes so I wiped them and then he was gone. I fell to my knees because at that moment, I knew that what I had done was wrong and my conscious was about to tear my mind apart. Every night I had a nightmare about my child. In some dreams, the child would be angry with me and I would wake up in a cold sweat crying and praying to God. But He never responded.

A month passed by and I had yet to hear from Michael and this hurt me so bad. I would call him but it would go straight to his voicemail. I even called his mother and she would never answer. I fell into depression. I felt as though I didn't have God or anyone. Ava would try to talk to me but my heart was so sore that I couldn't even talk to her. Then one night, I prayed, "God I'm sorry, I didn't know. I asked you to help me but you didn't answer. Please forgive me because I didn't understand what I was getting myself into. Have mercy on me. Talk to me, I can't breathe. I feel like I've been stripped...stripped of air and water. I need you so please forgive me. Say something please." But I heard nothing. "Take my life I don't want it anymore. I'm tire of having nightmares. I'm tired of feeling alone. If you don't take my life, I will lay here until you do." From that moment on, I stayed in my room for days. I didn't eat. I didn't sleep. Ava would come to my bedside and cry and beg me to talk to her but I wouldn't respond. My body would ache due to malnutrition but I didn't care. I just laid in my bed waiting on God to take my life away from me.

After so many days, Ava called my mom and told her about me. My mom then rushed over to the apartment. Seeing how frail I was she began to cry, "Baby Mommy is here. It's okay. I've come to take you home." I couldn't bear to look at my mom's face with tears in her eyes.

I whispered, "Mom."

She gasped with relief, "it's okay Angel. Let's go home."

I laid there as my mom and Ava gathered my things together. Bobby walked in the room. I noticed the look on his face as he looked at me with his hands over his mouth. My mom said to him, "It's alright. Just help me get her to the car."

They both picked me up and carried me to the car. Ava began to cry as Bobby was putting my feet in the car. Bobby kissed me on the cheek, "You better not let whatever it is win, fight Angel."

Mom and I drove off and headed home. She didn't ask me anything. We both were silent the whole ride there and the further we got away from the apartment, the better I felt.

We finally made it home. Mom helped me into the house once everything was settled. She sat down in front of me on my bed, "Baby, are you sick?"

"No." I could barely talk but with the little breath I did have I spoke with tears in my eyes, "But I don't want to live Mom."

"Angel I know life can be tough sometimes but God will make everything alright. Nothing is worth not wanting to live anymore. I don't care what you go through in life, nothing should ever want you to not live anymore, you hear me? Now we're going to get you up, take a shower, comb your hair, and get you something to eat because the devil will not win."

I did just as my mom said. As the days passed by, I began to get my strength back in my legs. I even gained some of my weight back. Being at home brought back so many memories. I thought about how I was so happy talking to

God and everything that he had taught me in my room. One night I sat up in my bed and whispered, "Jesus, are you there?" Like I did when I was little girl, but in those days he would respond. "If you are, I want to ask for your forgiveness and tell you I'm sorry and please talk to me. I need you. Please let me know that you have forgiven me because I'm truly sorry for everything…for turning my back on you, for being rebellious, and I promise that if I get pregnant again, I will not have another abortion no matter the circumstance because now I know it's wrong. Please forgive me."

That night I had a dream and in this dream I was playing in snow. Everything around me was pure white and someone walked up to me with a bouquet of beautiful white roses. I heard Jesus say, "**I'm here Angel. I was with you through it all so,**

> **'Come now, let us settle the matter,'**
> **said the LORD.**

'Though your sins are like scarlet,
they shall be as white as snow;
though they are red as crimson,
they shall be like wool. If you are willing and obedient,
you will eat the good things of the land;
but if you resist and rebel,
you will be devoured by the sword.'

Remember these words I say to you. I love you and I will always be with you. Your sins have been forgiven."

I woke up with a smile. Just hearing his voice alone felt so good. It felt as though I had been watered and I finally could breathe again.

Chapter Four

"Endurance"

Spring had arrived and my mom thought it would be a good idea for me not to complete the last semester of school and I agreed as well because I really didn't want to go back there and face my past. That was definitely something I wasn't ready for. Things became interesting at home. I had gained all of my weight back and I also became more active in the church. I was asked to be an assistant for one of Pastor Davis's aides and helped out in the nursery when needed. Ava was still at Western and she and Bobby would come and visit often. I never heard from Michael again. I guess he had meant what he said. I could slowly feel myself coming back to life again. I was even talking to God again daily in my room.

"Jesus, it's been nine months since everything happened and I have questions... I feel like I need to let this out...well I just want to know one thing."

"**What do you want to know?**" He asked.

"Why couldn't I hear you through it all? Why didn't you stop me? Where were you?"

"**I was there the whole time.**"

"Why didn't you answer any of my questions?"

"**I did, you asked for signs and signs I gave.**"

"But I didn't get the signs, I waited, I looked.

"**The first sign was through Michael, the second sign was the lady telling you to come into the church and talk about it, and the third sign was in the sonogram room when the lady asked you to see the baby knowing that if you saw what was on the inside of you, you wouldn't have had an abortion.**"

"How was I supposed to know all of this?"

"Angel I knew what your decision would be before the foundation of the world began. You chose not to see it because your mind was so far away from me. You wanted to see but because you were thinking about how it would affect others you couldn't see how it would affect you. What is done is done now I have a question for you."

"What's that?"

"Have you let it go?"

"I don't know. How can I? What I did was wrong."

"Yes it was and admitting that you were wrong is the first step to forgiveness. But healing, being able to let go and finding peace, completes the forgiving process and that Angel you have not done. I've forgiven you for what you have done because you admitted and asked for forgiveness for what you did, but you must let it go, and let all of

the hurt and regret go so that you can move forward."

I rubbed my head as tears fell from my eyes, "It's hard. I feel so bad Lord, it's like my insides are sore from hurt and my brain is swollen with regret."

"Go and get a towel to wash your face and get your mothers oil off of the countertop in the den." I then got up as the Lord instructed and walked back into my room. **"Now go and look into the mirror on your wall."** I looked at myself in the mirror. My eyes were red and filled with water. My nose was runny. **"Now tell her to let it go."**

I began to cry harder, "I can't." I turned away from myself in the mirror. "I feel like it's the only thing that I have left…the hurt…and I know that sounds crazy."

"No one should want to hold on to hurt Angel and I do know what you are saying. Oftentimes people feel like that is the only

thing that they have left to remember, but in reality, you gain nothing by doing so. There is no progression in hurt and in order to be happy and grow in me you must let go of the past. Now turn around Angel and tell her to let it go."

I turned back around slowly with the towel in my left hand and the bottle of oil in my right and I stared at myself for a couple of minutes, "Again I am sorry for what I have done, for the hurt I brought upon myself and tonight you, Angel Braveheart, will let this go. Jesus has forgiven you. Let it go."

"Now wash your face and anoint your head with oil." I did as he instructed and immediately felt so much better. A weight was lifted off my shoulders and even though I may never forget what I had been through, I thank the Lord for forgiving me and teaching me how to move forward despite the things I had done.

After that night, I could not understand why did Jesus love me so much? Why does he even care about someone like me? And how even himself would be able to forgive me? I thought of how rebellious I was and how at times I didn't even want him to talk to me. I felt so bad because I treated a man that I loved with such a level of disrespect and he loves me so much and was willing to stand beside me through it all and forgive me and help me move past my wrong doings. I thought there must be something that I could do for him. I pondered on what do you give someone that has everything? I then thought and thought and thought some more, "I got it!" I called out unto the Lord, "Lord!"

"I'm here."

"I want to let you know that I love you so much and I thank you for being my everything and I just want to show you how much I love you."

"Okay."

I proceeded to say while looking through my books on the bookshelf in my room, "Hold on just a second," I steadily looked through the books, "Okay I know you may know what I'm about to do but can you act surprised?"

"My eyes are shut."

"Alright well open them." In my hand was a dictionary. "Okay I asked myself, what could I give someone that has everything? And then it hit me, time. I have this dictionary because I thought it would be nice to know more about you."

"I love it Angel."

"Okay when I open the dictionary with my eyes closed and the first word that I see when I stop the pages will tell me what I look like to you."

"Alright"

I closed my eyes and felt the breeze from the pages turning in my hand and then I stopped, "Okay what do I look like to you?" I opened the dictionary and saw the word "speckle" a small dot. I laughed, "That's funny I'm that small that is amazing we look like speckles to you?"

"Yes you do."

"That is amazing. How are you able to distinguish all of us?"

"Even though you all look like speckles, each speckle does not look the same."

"Wow! Okay now…so how do you feel?" I closed my eyes and turned the pages and stopped and opened my eyes and saw the word 'exquisite'. I looked up towards the heavens, "And you should feel that way because you are awesome Jesus." After hours of me spending time with the Lord, I felt like I was on top of the world and if I wanted to fly I could. I felt so free I wanted to learn more about him and the more I spent time with the Lord, the more I saw things differently.

"So did you make sure that Pastor Davis has his water in his room on a napkin with a peppermint next to it?" said Tia, the head aide at church. I nodded, "Yes Tia"

"I just didn't want him to ask for it. We have to make sure that he has everything that he needs."

"Of course Tia I know you give me this speech every Sunday."

Tia was always on the edge when it came to Pastor Davis. It's almost as if she knew him more than anyone else in the congregation from the time he wakes up until he is fast asleep. "Tia,"

She pushed up her glasses, "Yes Angel?"

"I'm only asking a question."

"Okay"

"If you do everything for the Pastor then what does his wife do? I mean you do a lot!"

"Well Angel that's why I have you now."

She laughed, "Angel I don't do everything for the Pastor there are others that help him as well. Like his wife, she helps serve the people and attend to him at home." She proceeds and turns to me with a smirk on her face, "I know you see me doing a lot and you have questions but just know that when it comes to the Pastor and the Lady of the house, you do exactly what they say no matter what because they are our leaders and do a great job. And stop wondering in that little brain of yours and let's go and pray with the Ushers before service starts." While walking to the prayer room Tia continued, "You know it was Pastor Davis's idea for you to be my assistant."

I stopped walking and looked at her puzzled, "I was wondering why you asked me of all people. I'm only twenty years old and my organizational skills are not all that great."

"It will get there Angel. I'll make sure that it does."

"Well did he say why?"

She slowly turned to me, "The only thing he said was that he wanted you to work closely with him because he sees something in you."

"Hmmm okay that explains it."

"There is no time for sarcasm miss Angel," she opened the prayer room door.

When we walked into the prayer room, all of the Ushers on duty greeted each other, some were talking and laughing. I thought to myself that all this time I never knew that it was so lively in the prayer room with the Ushers. I then overheard a conversation from one of the Ushers saying, "Yes and don't you know that deacon West was caught coming out of the back with the woman?"

"Girl you lying," another said.

They proceeded to talk and one of them said, "Now let that had been one of us we would have been put off the Usher board!"

I had a startled look on my face to know that this is what had been going on all along in church? The head Usher on post called, "Let us all bow our heads with prayer." He then began to pray, "Many blessings and thank you to the Lord. In Jesus name amen."

I said with a loud voice, "And Lord please help deacon West and forgive the woman he got caught with in the back room and I pray that you continue to strengthen him and his family at this time."

There was a total silence in the room. I opened my eyes and everyone was staring at me with their mouths open. I looked around at them, "What? We can talk about it but we can't pray about it?"

The head Usher demanded, "Tia take her out of here."

Tia grabbed my arm tightly and pulled me out of the room, "Angel! Didn't I tell you to keep your thoughts and comments to yourself?"

"What did I do? It was a prayer."

"Yes a prayer that exposed a lot Angel, no one wanted to pray about deacon West and his mistress and everyone in the room didn't know about that."

"Okay I'm sorry for saying that out loud but I'm not sorry for praying for them. I just feel like if people would pray for others maybe they wouldn't do those things in the church."

"And you're the judge Angel."

"No I'm not but why gossip about it and not pray about it?"

Tia held up her finger at me, "You better hope Pastor don't find out about this, let's go."

All through service I could not rest. My spirit was leaping. I was so furious at the way people could gossip about things that go on in the church and don't want to expose it and pray about it as a church family. I said okay God when Pastor Davis does altar call I have to say something. Altar call was now in session. I heard the Lord say, **"Angel tell the truth."**

I got up after every one of us was prayed over. "Pastor, may I say something?" He then looked at me funny as though he didn't want to give me the microphone.

I said softly "Jesus" and it's almost as if the Lord released him to do so and he smiled, "Speak daughter."

I grabbed the mic, "Okay, I know that this is different." I saw Tia from a distance cover her face with her Bible. I proceeded. "But I have something to say."

I heard someone say, "Speak baby let him use you."

I nodded and smiled. "A while back I did something that I thought I would never have had to do or even dreamed of." I took a deep swallow, "I had an abortion. Now I know what some of you may be thinking, 'God hates me, or I'm going to hell' and some of you may even despise me after. After doing that I realized it was wrong. I have asked the Lord to forgive me and he has. Like many of you, before this, I prayed, I heard God, and yet like many of us, I rebelled as well. But I found out that through it all Jesus loves me. And how do I know this? I wanted to die afterwards. I wanted to die! I stopped eating. My mother didn't understand. My friends didn't understand. I would not speak a word to anyone. I lost weight. I was nothing but bones. But before I could even take a last breath, I knew he had to send the order. But instead, he sent my mother and she nursed me back to health. And not only that, but He spoke to me and told me that He loved me and forgave me. And because he did not take my life when I asked, because he spoke to me and told me he forgive me, that alone tells me that he loves me and he forgives me. Some of us in here, we talk about other people problems and we gossip about other people's trials, but we don't nurse them back to life with prayer. We don't cover them with the word…and we call ourselves a church family. What about exposing ourselves to help someone else! Now I'm not perfect and some of you may say that I don't understand but at the end of the day, what I have learned is that prayer ain't never hurt nobody, the Word has never failed, and Jesus will always be Lord, not us."

The whole church was in an up roar. People were yelling, "Praise the Lord! And hallelujah! You let him used you baby!"

Pastor Davis hugged me so tightly, "I love you daughter."

I felt warmth come over me and tears began to fall from my eyes. I heard Jesus say, **"I'm proud of you, well done."**

After church, my mom and I went to my grandmother's house. On the way there, my mom was very quiet, and quickly broke the silence, "It was a good service today wasn't it." I looked out of the window, "Yes ma'am it was."

My mom pulled over on the side of the road and put the car in park. "Angel I just want you to know that what you did at church today was very, very brave and that I love you."

"I love you too mom... so what is the but," I always knew that when my mother said she loved me that there was a but somewhere for a warning or for a deep conversation.

She looked at me with a smile, "The but is that yes, people cheered at the truth and they shouted a lot and praised the Lord, but baby don't think that everyone really grasped what

God was saying. Some people will use your deliverance against you."

"I don't understand."

She grabbed my hand. "You will one day but I want you to know this, that no matter what happens, you pray and you ask the Lord to strengthen you no matter how hard it gets and be strong."

I looked at her, "Yes' ma'am I will."

Mom put the car in drive and we continued to grandma's house.

"There is my baby!" My grandmother yelled, "Come here my little Angel."

Grandma always held a special place in my heart and even though a lot of times she would get on to me and other family members, we knew to straighten up because granny did not play. Grandma looked at me after hugging me close with her small gray eyes and big glasses, "I just got a phone call about how you gave an excellent testimony in service at your church today!"

"Yeah I couldn't help myself."

"I wish I could have been there to hear it."

Suddenly the door opened and in walked Aunt Missy loud and obnoxious self, "Well y'all could have told me that you all were leaving. I was looking for you both after service was over."

"Oh we left as soon as Angel finished with Tia in the office," my mother explained.

"Angel," Aunt Missy turned to me, "I've been meaning to ask you do they pay you at the church to be Tia's assistant?"

"No why should they?"

"Please! I could not be walking behind Tia all day and not be getting paid."

"Well I don't think that Tia should be getting paid to do something that she is supposed to do anyways," Grandma replied.

"Yeah, but that gal work honey. She pretty much runs the whole church."

My mother changed the subject, "How have you been mama?"

And before Grandma could open her mouth Aunt Missy then interrupted, "She's fine Joanne can't you see that? Anyways, Angel back to you!"

Mom murmured under her voice, "Here we go."

"Yes here we go. See that's why your daughter got up and told her business to the whole church and I'm sure it was nothing you knew about!"

"Does that matter to you Missy?!" my mom exclaimed.

"No, I actually enjoyed Angel today even though I disagree with some stuff she said."

"Disagree?" my mom placed one of her hands on her hips.

"Yes, I disagreed."

"Okay Aunt Missy what is it that you disagree with?" I asked.

She looked at my mom then looked at me, "Well I'm going to tell you the truth since your momma don't want to tell you."

"Okay"

"You looked like a fool up there telling everyone how you got rid of a baby and how you tried to kill yourself. Complete nonsense, and when the last time you ever heard God forgiving someone for that, you going straight to hell."

I looked at Aunt Missy with fire in my eyes and I looked at my mother and bit my tongue, "Excuse me." and walked out of the room.

"You are the most evil person I know," Mom told Missy. "Angel!" My mom yelled for me.

I could hear her and Aunt Missy going back and forth and grandmother trying to make peace. I remembered what my mom said in the car about how people will use your deliverance against you and to be strong. I walked back into the room, "Stop it! Stop it!" There became total silence in the room. "Aunt Missy before you say anything else to me in any type of matter I want you to clean off the things on your list." She looked at me with her head sideways and with a look like 'no she did not' on her face, "Yes your list and let us not get started on it but if you want to we can. Now the last time I checked the Lord died for all sins and not only that, he turned uneducated people and murders and thieves into Christians that served him and he used them. And not to add they all had stories and they all went through something and I didn't find any of their stories to be embarrassing and they certainly were not made out to be fools. So if you want to point the finger and use what God has brought me out of to throw it in my face then that's on you because I will not sit here and entertain it. And if I do go to heaven or hell you won't be the one that put me in either. I've taken a whole lot of things from you and I have bitten my tongue every single time out of respect. All I ask in return is for you to have some for me."

Aunt Missy looked at me in anger, "I will never have respect for a child, children respect me! And you all are okay with this child talking to me like she a grown woman?"

"She is grown and she's right. I read the Bible." Grandma said.

Mom shook her head in agreement, "Missy right is right."

Aunt Missy looked around at all of us, "Well I'll be, I never thought that I would see this day coming where y'all would gang up on me!"

"Nobody is ganging up on you," Mom told her.

Aunt Missy huffed, "Well I guess it's time for me to go," and grabbed her things as she got up from the sofa.

Grandmother yelled, "The Bible was right!"

Right about what Mama?" Mom asked.

"If you resist the devil, he will flee from you." We all laughed, well except for Aunt Missy who became furious and walked out and slammed the door. Grandmother smiled at me, "She will be alright, and Angel don't you worry about what people think, if God move you to do something, you do it."

My mother concurred, "Amen."

That next week I felt the urge to study my Bible even more. I wanted to know more about being anointed. I asked God to teach me what it was to be anointed and what the anointing was, "Lord you told me I was anointed. What is that and how did this all happen?"

"I'm going to tell you in a way that you would understand so you won't need your

dictionary for this one. To be anointed means that you hold an office to a higher purpose in life. You were chosen and destined to do my will. The anointing is my presence that covers you and gives you the power to do my will. Go get your Bible." I did just as the Lord said, **"Turn to John 2:27."**

I read it out loud, "As for you, the anointing you received from him remains in you, and you do not need anyone to teach you. But as his anointing teaches you about all things and as that anointing is real, not counterfeit—just as it has taught you, remain in him…Wow!"

"So you see Angel I am with you. My residue is on you. You have already been equipped, now you must be taught by what is in you."

"Okay so let me get this straight, you're going to teach me how to be me, through me?"

He laughed, **"You can say that, however it's not you teaching you, it is the anointing that I have given you that will teach you."**

"Okay, what now?"

"Angel my love our next stop is purpose."

Days and months passed by and I would stay up in the wee hours of the night studying and writing down everything that the Lord spoke to me. And then one night as I was sitting on my bed with my bible in front of me reading, my Bible began to thump. I rubbed my eyes because I thought that I was getting a little tired from the studying. But it thumped again. I jumped back and realized that my Bible was beating like a heart. I rubbed my eyes again and blue and red veins began to connect the words and it continued to thump faster and faster. I saw a heart and gasped, "Oh my God, my Bible is alive!"

"It's okay Angel!"

"Okay I'm freaking out here, what is going on?"

"It's okay."

"Okay what just happened?"

"The Word became real to you."

"I didn't know the Bible was alive. I mean it had veins and a heart and it was beating."

"The Bible is real and very much so alive Angel."

I looked at the Bible again but everything was gone. "Why did it do that?"

"Because your heart was in it."

"Okay is there anything else I need to know about before I get another surprise and freak out like I just did? I mean that was a lot."

"You will learn as you go and the Word is your weapon, it's a powerful tool and the more you use it the more battles you win. Now get some rest." I felt an embrace of cool air touch my body and I fell asleep.

After studying the word of God, everything started to look different to me in church and after the testimony I gave, a lot of old and young people began to give their testimonies. And at home I would be taught by the Holy Spirit every night. I would study and Sunday morning when Pastor Davis would get up and speak, he would begin to preach about the things the Lord was teaching me in private. It became almost as though I knew every Sunday what Pastor Davis was preaching. I also noticed that I had gotten way ahead and that sometimes he would preach things that weren't current until it became current to him.

"Angel!" Tia yelled through the crowd after church, "Pastor Davis would like to speak with you in his office."

"Okay," I replied. 'What could he possibly want with me,' I thought. I knocked on the door of the Pastor's Study.

"Come in," Pastor Davis said cheerfully. "Daughter, I see that Tia told you what I said."

"Yes sir she did, and do you need anything?"

"No I just want to have a word with you. I didn't get a chance to tell you how powerful your testimony was and how I have seen the church grow since then. Young lady you have a gift."

"Well praise the Lord Pastor."

"I just want you to be encouraged and to know that if you need anything my door is always open."

"Well... Pastor Davis, there is one thing."

He looked at me with a surprised look on his face, "What's that?"

"Before I went off to college, the Lord told me that I was anointed to preach and for months now I have been taught by him. I don't know when I will be ready or when will he finish teaching me but I do know what he has told me."

Pastor Davis looked at me with a serious look on his face, "Are you sure Angel?"

"I'm positive Pastor, at first I didn't want to do it. I ran from it but when I saw how much the Lord loves me I knew that I had to do whatever it is that he wants me to do. I was afraid because I thought that he would not be with me. I even doubted what he told me, but I could not shake it nor run from it anymore."

Pastor Davis rubbed his head, "Okay I believe you but I'm going to have to pray about this Angel, and I want you to pray as well, and whatever I come back and tell you know that it is out of love and that it is what the Lord wants."

"Okay Pastor, I will pray and I'm not worried because I already know what he is going to say." I got up and said, "Have great day Pastor and may God bless you."

"Same to you daughter, God bless you."

That night while going over scriptures with the Holy Spirit I stopped, "Lord,"

"Yes Angel."

"I…"

"I don't mean to cut you off Angel, but I know what you are going to say and I don't want you to worry your pretty little self about what Pastor Davis is going to say."

"But I'm nervous even though I know that you are going to tell him who I am. What if he doesn't accept it because I'm young or what others may think?"

"Angel who can stop the Lord; what does my word say?"

"If God be for you, who can be against you."

"Right!"

"I'm just curious Lord, what will you say to him?"

"Your Pastor could be stubborn at times Angel, so I know that I would have to pay him a visit."

"Pay him a visit?"

"Yes, he will tell you about it. You will see."

The next Sunday morning I really didn't think about what I had told Pastor Davis but he sure did think about it. As soon as I walked through the church doors, he had Tia to find me before service and bring me to his office. His wife was sitting on the sofa by the door and he was standing up with his hands on his head.

"Good morning," I said to them both with a smile.

His wife greeted, "Hey Angel how are you?"

"I'm good and you?"

She smiled, "I'm wonderful baby."

My Pastor sat down, "Angel have a seat."

"What's up?"

"I have been awake since 2 am this morning."

"You have Pastor?"

"Yes I have and do you know why?"

I immediately thought about what the Lord had told me the week before, "I may have an idea."

"I had a dream Angel and in that dream the Lord was with me and he spoke to me concerning you."

"Okay what did he say?"

He looked at me seriously and cleared his throat, "He told me that you are anointed to preach the Gospel and to put you up there and if I did not obey him he will deal with me."

I swallowed deeply, "Oh my."

"I know it was him Angel because I never had a dream like this before, it was so real." He continued, "Now I have spoken with the board and let me tell you, Mrs. Agnew they accept her because she is an elder, but with you they had a major problem with. For one, because you are a female and two, because they felt as though you were too young. But I told them I could not disobey God and after going back and forth with them they came to their senses and said that it was okay."

I smiled with joy, " Pastor I don't know what to say."

Lady Davis said, "Say Hallelujah!"

"Hallelujah! God is good!"

"Yes he is," Lady Davis replied, "he's more than good! I'm so excited Angel. When my husband told me this I instantly felt it in my spirit that it was the right thing. I told him that I wish I could be that bold and that I have always wanted God to call me, but he hasn't, but I am thankful that he has chosen you baby."

Pastor Davis smiled, "Yes we are thankful, so thankful, now let us pray." We all bowed our heads for a word of prayer.

After prayer, Pastor Davis informed, "I'm not going to announce it today because I want the Lord to continue what he is doing in you. Stay close to me and pay attention, this will help you with presentation. I can't teach you how to preach Angel, that's not my job, it's his and I will not put my hands on that area. But as a Pastor, I must show you how to present yourself and be a leader."

"Yes sir,"

"Has the Lord given you a date?"

I thought, "A date?"

The Lord whispered, **"The first Sunday in June."**

I answered, "The first Sunday in June."

"Okay and you're sure Angel?"

I smiled, "I'm sure."

"Okay well that's alright." He begin writing it down on his calendar. He looked at the calendar, "That's only four months away!"

"Yep it is."

"I will announce it a month before, how about that?"

"That would be great!'

"Okay, sounds like service has started, you two better go into the sanctuary." Lady Davis and I then left the office.

When I arrived home, I ran to my room, "Okay God we have four months."

"Correction Angel, we have a lifetime."

"Yes a lifetime."

There were so many things to learn about life and I realized that the Bible is our life's manual. Everything that I ever wanted to know about life from being in love, from habits, I learned about them through the Lord's word. I was so excited to learn something new that it had gotten to the point to where I had forgot about the world. I would study for eight hours and sometimes ten a day. I carried the word with me wherever I went. I would pray and speak healing over those who were sick just as I read that Jesus did. I even saw them be healed right before my eyes. Every Sunday, the Pastor would have me to come down to the altar at altar call to pray over people and I did as I was told. At times I would pray until my face became pale. And often times I would fast for so long that even the Lord would tell me it is time to eat.

The first Sunday in June had finally arrived and I was so nervous. I could feel my heart racing and beating exceedingly fast. "Angel!" My mom yelled, "You have thirty minutes to get dressed because we have to go."

"Yes ma'am I'm almost done." While buttoning up my blouse I shouted, "Jesus, today is the day!"

"Yes it is, do not be nervous because I will be with you the entire time."

I smiled, "From start to finish?"

"From the beginning to the end,"

"You promise?"

"You have my word."

I was now officially ready to go to the church. "Come on Angel, let's go, you don't want to be late to your first sermon."

"I know mom,"

We finally got into the car. "Do you have everything Angel?"

"Yep I do."

Mom cranked up the car, "Well let's go,"

When we arrived at the church there were so many people that we couldn't even find a parking spot. "Well it looks like a lot of people have come to hear the Lord speak through you today Angel. It's just three forty five and the service doesn't start until four."

I swallowed hard because it felt as though my heart was about to jump out of my mouth. An outdoor usher told my mom to park in the front beside the Pastor. As soon as we parked, I blurted, "Mommy?"

She looked startled, "Oh no Angel, I know you not about to change your mind."

"No I'm not going to do that. I just wanted you to pray with me before we go in."

She smiled, "Okay."

We held hands as I prayed, "Heavenly Father thank you for this day and thank you for your people who have come out to hear your word Father, with your word may lives be changed and minds be renewed and the sick recover and be healed, and thank you in advance for everything in Jesus name, Amen."

Mom had tears in her eyes, "Okay I'm not going to cry but I just want you to know that I am so proud of you baby. I am and I will be praying for you while you are up there, and if you get nervous just look at me and ask God to help you, okay?"

"I will Mom."

We got out of the car and began to walk to the Pastor's Study. Tia greeted us with a smile, "Are you ready Angel?"

I smiled, "Yep as long as I have Jesus I will be alright."

"Amen. Well let me get your things and you and your mom can follow me."

We walked through the doors of the Pastor study and there were so many preachers in the study. Pastor Davis stated, "There she is. Angel, come on in take a seat in my chair." Everyone in the room stood at attention as I walked in the room and gave me hugs and shook my hand. He then said, "Everyone this is Angel. I'm sure you all have heard great things about this powerful vessel of God."

Everyone smiled and said, "Yes we have."

They all went around the room and told me their names and where they were from. I smiled, "This is so wonderful for you all who don't even know me to come out and support me." They all replied that I was most welcome.

The time was now four o'clock and I could hear the roaring of the congregation praising the Lord. Pastor Davis said, "Well it sounds like service is stirring up, can we all have a moment of prayer and also a moment of silence for Sister Jones who lost her mother on yesterday." We all stood up and bowed our heads and had a moment of silence. Pastor Davis began to pray. After the prayer and sitting in the Pastor Study for fifteen minutes it was now time for us to walk into the sanctuary. I could see my heartbeat on my shirt. Pastor Davis turned to us, "We will line up in the order I place you." He lined us up and I was last. He looked at me, "Okay Angel, it's Showtime, are you ready?"

"Yes sir, I'm ready." I looked up and took a deep breath and exhaled slowly and looked up and said under my voice, "from start to finish."

I heard the Lord say, **"From the beginning to the end."**

We all walked into the sanctuary one by one. When I walked in, people were smiling and shouting and praising God. We all sat on the first pew in front of the congregation. It was so many people there. I never thought anyone cared enough to come. I thought it was going to be me a few members, my mom, and the Pastor and his wife. I looked over my shoulder and saw half of my family. I was filled with joy.

That day I preached "Look at what he did for you". It came from Luke 19 about how Jesus was trialed and crucified for our sins. And that any time you ever get to your lowest points in your life, you should go back and get your Bible and look at what he did for you. I also talked about how Job was tested and even though he went through many trials and hit the lowest point in his life, he still referred back to what he knew about the Lord and that alone gave him the strength to endure his trials and overcome them and receive his blessing. Many of us have given up in those trials to the extent of committing suicide or spiritual suicide by turning our backs on God, but it's something about going back and looking at what he did for you. It stirs up your spirit, enhances your faith, gives you peace, and lets you know that you are loved and needed in the body of Christ. Because not only did He die for your sins, but He also died so that His spirit could dwell in us to teach us how to live right and remind us of not just who we are, but whose we are.

After I was used by the Lord, I heard Him say, **"Well done Angel. I love you so much. "**

"I love you too," I replied as I sat down in my seat. I felt such an indescribable feeling of happiness embracing me that I had to shout out and cry out to God with Praise. The whole church continued clapping, shouting, leaping, and sending Praises to God.

Pastor Davis asked me so many questions after everything had calmed down and had me to elevate my right hand and on that day I was given a license and I was ordained as a minister of the Gospel.

Chapter Five

"Grace"

Years had passed by since I had become a minister of the Gospel. I was now twenty five years old. I had seen a lot in the church: people disagreeing and causing confusion; family against family; and even people getting upset with Pastor Davis and leaving the church. I would only hear little of it because I had begun to travel from city to city and state to state preaching the word of the Lord. I met so many people and so many Pastors that I had lost count and couldn't list all the names of the places I had gone. My itinerary was always booked from January until December. I saw that God was using me mightily and I was excited about the things that God was doing in my life. Even though I was blessed with engagements and doing the will of God, my life began to follow a path that I was not ready for.

While sitting in Pastor Davis' office I was wondering as to why he had called me to come visit him. Suddenly the door opened and it was Pastor Davis, "Girl you back I see. I have been hearing some wonderful things and I have seen how the Lord is using you." While walking to his seat he continued, "But Angel," he sat down and positioned himself to where he was comfortable, "I think it is time for me to let you go."

"Let me go?" I asked shockingly,

"If I keep you here Angel, it would only keep you from where you are headed. Angel I know the anointing that God has placed on your life. I have seen what he has done through you and you need to be somewhere that God can take you out so that the world can hear you."

"But Pastor I don't understand."

"If you are okay with speaking to a hundred people here and two hundred people there Angel, that's fine if that is something that you are content with. But if you want to take your ministry to nations, then child that won't happen here. You were destined to speak to nations about the word of God."

"But Pastor where will I go?"

"Don't worry, I have already talked to a Pastor that I know that would be glad to allow you to be on his ministerial staff. Do you know Pastor Rowland Peers?"

"Yes, I have heard of him."

"Well he has the largest ministry in this great state of Kentucky,"

"Oh yeah the guy that sings funny."

He laughed, "Yes him. He and his wife would like to meet with you."

"Okay when?"

"This Wednesday at their church…it's called 'The Agape Church' over on Clinton Avenue."

"It's at seven?"

"No, six and they would like to talk to you afterwards. Now they are some very well-known people and I would not send you over there if I did not feel good about it. But I have to release you because of the anointing that you carry so that you can see something that is greater than you."

"Okay Pastor I'll go."

"Good, I will give him a call to let him know you are coming. In the meantime, pray, be faithful, listen to your Pastor, and always trust in the Lord."

"I will," I walked out of the door.

While driving home I asked Jesus, "Lord, how do you feel about this? My Pastor is asking me to join another ministry, what about help grow the ministry where I am? I mean isn't that what it is all about?"

"Angel I think you overlooked everything that he was trying to get you to understand."

"But why me, and not one of his other protégés, such as Jimmy? I like where I am."

"You are not Jimmy and Jimmy is not you. This is all a part of your journey. Remember when I told you that our next stop is purpose?"

"Yes Lord, I remember."

"Well we are in the purpose part of your life now and our next stop is destiny."

"Okay, I will follow you wherever you go Lord and do whatever you want me to do."

"Okay, destiny it is."

"From start to finish,"

"From beginning until the end."

Wednesday had arrived and I must say that I wasn't too excited about walking into a new ministry. I would have to learn about their ministry and meet totally different people. But if this was the place that the Lord wanted me to be, then I was definitely ready for it.

On my way to the church, I began to talk to the Lord, "Lord, I am nervous about this. I'm nervous because I don't know what I am about to walk into."

"I know Angel, but know that I am with you." I pulled into the parking lot of the church, **"Angel before you get out of the car, there is something that I must tell you."**

"Yes Lord?"

"You must know that you will only be here for a season and when it is time to go you must leave."

"Okay God I will."

I got out of the car and the church seemed so far away from the parking lot. The building was huge. It was bigger than any church I had ever seen before. There were lights that led all the way up to the parking lot. The grass was cut so neatly. I saw people who had a handicap on a flat escalator that took them to the front of the building while I walked alongside them on the neatly paved sidewalk. I walked through the doors and the sanctuary was beautiful and there were eight people singing and worshiping the Lord. I immediately felt the presence of the Lord. There was a very sweet anointing in the church. I was greeted by so many people and even though I couldn't sit closer to the platform, I was okay with being far away from it because Jesus was everywhere in the church. Pastor Peers then got up and began to teach about Love. He taught us that Love covers a multitude of sins. He also taught us that without love, how could there even be any of us? Because didn't God so love the world that he gave his only begotten son so that we may have life? It was a great teaching and when it was over he asked, "Is Minister Angel Braveheart here?" Everyone looked around and I slowly raised my hand. "Come down here just for a second Angel." I got up and walked down towards the platform. I could feel my heart racing a thousand times. I felt the eyes of the people watching me walk. Pastor Peers then said to the congregation, "Y'all give her a hand as she comes." The people began to clap. When I stood before him he informed, "Angel is one of our newest members. She was sent here by her Pastor." He looked to his wife, "Pam come here for a second honey and bring the oil." His wife got up and got the oil, "Now I want you to know that the Agape church family and I and my wife welcome you. The Lord has anointed you to preach the gospel and just like the ministers on my staff you will serve the Lord in doing that and much more. I'm going to lay hands on you because the Lord is about to release a fresh oil upon your life. The anointing shall be on you strong and you will begin to operate in every gift that the Lord has given you." He then directed me saying, "Lift your hands." I lifted my hands. "Angel Braveheart, you are a Prophetess to the nations. You will travel the world and preach the Gospel. You will lay hands on the sick and they shall recover. You shall Prophecy and everything you say shall be made manifest in the name of Jesus!" He touched my hands as his wife touched my stomach. I felt a strong embrace of the Holy Spirit cover me and all I remember was waking up with a sheet over my face.

I got up and an older woman grabbed my hand and gave me a hug, "May God bless you baby."

"You as well," I replied.

I felt a little weak, but the more I stood there I could feel my strength coming back to me. I saw Pastor Peers walking through the crowd of people while greeting them and coming towards me. Finally he walked up and hugged me and looked at me, "You good?"

"Yes I am."

He laughed, "It's good to see you."

"You as well Pastor Peers."

"Well, one of my ushers is going to take you to my office. My wife and I will be there shortly."

"Okay."

He raised his hand and called for a big, heavyset guy who stood over six feet tall with curly hair and a brown complexion, "Fred! Fred!" Fred came to where the Pastor and I were standing "Can you please escort this young lady to my office and stay with her until I get there."

"Yes sir," Fred turned to me, "Angel is it?"

"Yes it is."

"Follow me."

We walked through the crowd and down a hallway. We finally entered this gigantic room with a television and brown leather sofas.

There were a lot of certificates on the walls with Pastor Peers' name on them so I asked Fred, "Are all of these the Pastor's?"

"Yeah they are."

"Wow he did a lot."

Fred laughed, "Yeah he's a great man of God."

"Yes," I said, "I can see all of his accomplishments on the wall."

We both laughed, Pastor and his wife walked in. Mrs. Peers was so beautiful; she had a glow about her and a beautiful smile. She walked up to me, "Welcome daughter."

"Thank you Lady Peers."

Pastor Peers shook Fred's hand, "Thank you Fred I really appreciate it."

"No problem Pastor anytime," he walked out of the door.

Pastor Peers walked around the sofa, "Please Angel take a seat, do you want anything to drink?"

"Water would be nice."

"Water it is," he said and looked to his wife, "What about you dear?"

Lady Peers held her hand up, "I'm fine."

Pastor Peers handed me a bottle of water, "So Angel, did you enjoy the teaching?"

"Yes sir I did."

"Well good, I didn't make you feel uncomfortable did I?"

"No you didn't at all, even though I was a little nervous."

He laughed, "Awe I'm sorry but I had to do what God said do."

"I understand that," "Are all of these people your members?"

"Yes, all 17,000 souls and counting."

"Wow! That is amazing."

"Yes and I thank God for each one. I have a great church family and you are now a part of it."

All I could think of to say was "Wow!"

"We have heard so many great things about you Angel."

"You have?"

"Yes"

Then his wife nodded, "Yes we have."

He continued, "When your Pastor called me, I knew that it was about you. You are a powerful young woman girl!"

"Well Praise God!" I shouted.

"Angel, I know that this may be a lot different from what you are use to and it may take a while for you to adjust so I want you to walk with this lady right here, my wife, she will take good care of you."

"Okay I will,"

"So stick to her like glue, exchange numbers, talk with her, get to know one another."

"Okay," I looked at his wife as she smiled.

She reached in her purse, "Angel I'm going to give you my card." She handed it to me.

"Okay thank you Lady Peers."

Pastor Peers gave me his card, "And here is mine. I wrote my personal number on the back."

"Okay." I replied.

"Feel free to use those numbers anytime," he said, "Now what do you like to do in ministry Angel, besides preaching? We have over 150 ministries, name one or if God has given you one to bring to the church, let us know and we will get started on it right away."

"Wherever you place me Pastor, I am fine."

"Okay I would love for you to do outreach because I can see you flourishing in that area."

"Okay"

"I'm going to introduce you to Sister Lottie. She will get you started on first time member's orientation and connect you with Brother Lyles who is over the outreach ministry. Is that okay?"

"Yes"

"Good, alright are you ready Angel?"

"I'm ready!"

"Okay let us pray before you leave."

We all bowed our heads and Pastor Peers prayed aloud. After the prayer, we went our separate ways. There were still people in the parking lot as I walked to my car. I got into my car and drove home.

After a while of being there and working in the ministry, the Lord began to use me like never before. Everything that Pastor Peers had prayed over me had come to past. I could feel the anointing weighing heavy on me and I could see the glory of God moving through every ministry. Even though I missed my old church, I knew that God was doing something amazing in my life and the more he showed himself through me, the more life became challenging.

"Knock, knock," my mom said while knocking on my bedroom door.

"Come in."

Mom walked in, "What are you doing?

"I'm just studying, what's up?"

She sat on the bed, "Okay you know things have gotten a little tough for me lately with the bills."

"Yeah Mom, I know."

"Okay, well it looks like you are going to have to get a job to help out."

"But Mom I have the ministry and a lot of stuff going on."

My mom looked at me, "I know baby but you are twenty five years old and it is past time for you to learn some responsibility."

"But what about the money God has blessed me with through the ministry?"

"Angel that money is gone."

"All of it?"

"Yes all of it."

"Okay I'll look for a job tomorrow."

"Now baby I don't want you to think I'm trying to stop you from doing what God wants you to do, but I need you to understand that in order for us to live, we must eat, and to do that we need money and you need a job. I have carried you long enough, it's time."

"I understand Mom and one day I promise you won't have to work again."

She then laughed, "Yeah I wish."

"But it's true mom."

"Okay Angel, but remember what I said."

"Yes ma'am."

I slowly placed the bible over my face, "Jesus."

"Yes Angel."

"What is going on?"

"You tell me,"

"I just joined this ministry, how in the world am I going to find a job that will give me the flexibility that I need?"

"There is one. Go to the dental office on Main Street and put in an application. The owner is a man of God. He will understand."

"What will I do at a dentist office?"

"It's a job there with your name on it. Now go first thing in the morning."

"Okay I will."

The next morning, as I got ready to go, I heard the Lord say, **"Business casual."**

"This isn't business casual?"

"No, it is not. Instead of jeans and a blouse, put on a skirt and some heels with the blouse."

"Okay"

"Okay, do you have a resume?"

"Yep I have an old one."

"Update it before you go."

"I don't think working at the video game rental will help me that much."

"Angel"

"Okay Lord," I updated my resume.

"Okay Angel, now you may go. You look beautiful."

"Well thank you," I walked out of the door.

When I arrived to the dentist office, I walked up to the front desk and said to the lady sitting at the desk, "Hello my name is Angel and…"

She interrupted me, "Do you have an appointment?"

"No."

"Well go home, make one, and come back."

"I'm sorry but I am here to put in an application."

She looked at me weird, "Uh wait here."

I saw a tall man come from the back wearing a white coat with papers in his hand. He looked at me with a smile, "Hello can I help you?"

"Yes my name is Angel and I am here to apply for whatever position that you have available."

He put on a more serious face, "Okay well right now I have already filled the one that was available."

"Okay is there something else that you may have."

He reaffirmed, "I'm sorry but I don't have any more openings."

"May I ask, what was the position that was filled?"

"Sitting here at the front desk."

"Okay but someone told me to come here."

He looked towards the back, "Someone told you to come here?"

"Yeah, but it's okay."

All of a sudden his faced changed as though something had hit him. "Wait a minute. I may have something available just for you." He smiled and looked at some papers and looked up at me, "How would you like to assist me?"

"But I don't know anything about being a dentist,"

"Well I'll teach you. Your first day starts now."

I looked up at him with joy in my eyes, "What about the application?"

"We'll do that later. Come on back."

I was so happy. I could not take the smile off my face. I looked up while walking towards the back whispering, "Thank you Jesus!"

The lady at the desk looked kind of upset, but I was so excited. He took me to his office and turned to me, "Okay I didn't properly introduce myself but my name is Robert Jenkins, you can call me Dr. Rob. "And your name again is…"

"Angel, my name is Angel…Angel Braveheart."

Okay Angel, today I will teach you how to be the perfect dental assistant. Now there will be tests involved so pay attention closely every day."

"I will and thank you so much I really appreciate it."

I learned so much in that one day about being a dental assistant that my head was full. I could not wait to get home and tell my mom the wonderful news. "Mom!"

"I'm in the kitchen Angel!"

I walked into the kitchen while glowing with elation, "You are now looking at a dental assistant."

"Angel, no way!"

"Yes Mom!"

"How did that happen? You didn't go to school to be a dental assistant."

"Mom it was all Jesus. He told me to go and I went and got a job! God is so good!"

"Yes he is, I'm so happy for you...and oh yeah, by the way your Pastor called."

I placed my hand over my head, "Oh my goodness outreach! Mom what time is it?"

"It's six,"

"Okay mom I got to go. I'll see you in a little bit!" I rushed back out the door.

"Okay be careful," she yelled.

Today was the day that we had to do outreach within a local nearby community that was pretty rough. There are usually drug dealers, prostitutes, and drug users everywhere. We all load up a church bus to get there and once we arrive, we'd give them food, pray for them, and invite them to church. Some would accept our invitation and come, while others would say that they would but we never saw them. I loved going though. Everything about it was in line with what God desires from his people. He wants us to go out and minister his word and feed and clothe those who are less fortunate.

I was so excited about where I was in God. I had a job that was flexible and I was in a happy place. I began to receive so many more engagements but often times Pastor Peers would not allow me to go. He would say that it was because some people would try to prostitute the anointing to make money. I understood what he meant but at times I really wanted to go. The Lady of the church and I had also become really close. Overall, I was really happy with the way things were.

It was now preparation time at Agape Church to host its annual weeklong conference, The Agape Conference of Praise. It is the largest conference in the state. People of all races and color would come from around the world every year to join together and worship and receive the word of God at the conference. There are usually eight powerful men and women of God ministering at night and over a hundred teaching classes during the day. I was so excited because I had never experienced anything like it before and to finally hear in-person some of the ministers that I would watch on television made it even more exciting. I was so ready to worship and receive the word that God had for his people that I fasted and prayed for ten days leading up to the conference. I prayed about everything and the only thing I wanted to do was to hear the word of God through his servants.

During the week of the conference it was so busy. People were flying in from everywhere.

The hotels were filled to capacity insomuch that some of the church members had to invite some people to their homes to stay for that week. I had to invite a young lady named Kenya to come and stay with me and my Mom. Kenya seemed to be a very nice young lady. She was tall, thin and her skin complexion was hazelnut brown. She had blonde, pink, and green hair which was kind of weird. However, I was like if she likes it, I love it. The first night she came, I didn't know what to expect. She came off as a little weird until she began to tell me about everything that she had gone through. She was once homeless and had lived on her own ever since she was twelve. She didn't know who her real parents were and most of her years she was in foster care. She told me about how the Lord kept her away from drug use and how she had to dedicate her life fully to Christ because if had it not been for him she probably would not be alive today. After going to the conference that week and talking with Kenya, I realized that there are many people that have had her same situation. After hearing a lot of the stories in the classrooms, I realized that conferences are very much in need. There are a lot of hurting people that want to be poured into with the word of God. Kenya and I had become the best of friends by Wednesday night. However, unbeknownst to either me or Kenya, Wednesday night would also mark the point in which my life had begun to take a turn.

"Minister Braveheart," Pastor Peers yelled as he came out of his office, "I need you to do something for me please."

"Yes Pastor," "What is it that you need?"

"I need you to serve one of the speakers tonight, the Reverend Jim Strong."

"Okay"

"Make sure that he has water or if he needs anything before he goes on tonight. Billy will be the armor bearer but while he's in the office, I want you to make sure that he has everything that he needs."

"Yes sir, I will."

It was almost time for service to begin so I walked into the room where the speaker and other young ministers were gathering. "Hello everyone I'm Angel Braveheart," I said as I walked into the office, "Is everyone alright? Pastor Strong do you need anything?"

Pastor Strong just looked at me as though he was in a daze, he shook his head, "I'm sorry, but no thank you. I'm good."

"Anyone else?"

Everyone said that they were fine. The room had become silent where previously everyone had been talking to one another. "Well I'll be going. Pastor Strong if there is anything that you need before you preach, just let me know. I will be in the hospitality office next door until service begins."

Pastor Strong lifted up his head, "I will and thank you Angel"

"No problem," I walked out the room, and closed the door behind me.

As I sat in the hospitality office until service began, I heard a knock on the door. "Come in." To my surprise it was Pastor Strong. "Is everything okay Pastor Strong?"

"Oh no Angel everything is fine."

"Okay Pastor may I help you with something?"

"Has anyone ever told you that you were amazingly beautiful?"

I sighed, "Pastor Strong, are you trying to hit on me?"

He laughed, "Is that what you call it?"

"Yes it is."

He laughed again and sat on the desk, "Well Angel I am."

"But aren't you married?"

"Divorced, eight years now"

"I'm sorry to hear that."

"Oh that's no problem," He looked at the flat screen security monitors as Pastor Peers was coming to get him.

"Well it looks as though the people's hearts are ready for you now."

He looked at me, "But I'm ready for you Angel."

I looked at him and suddenly Pastor Peers entered the office clearing his throat, "Are you okay Pastor Strong?"

"I'm fine I was just asking this young lady about a couple of things."

Pastor Peers had a disturbed look on his face and looked at Pastor Strong upside the head "I see, well did she answer all of your questions?"

Pastor Strong smiled, "Not all of them, but let's go now shall we, the people are ready for the word of God."

They walked out of the door. I heard footsteps walking back towards the office as I had begun to gather my things. Pastor Peers came back into the room, "Angel are you okay?"

"I'm fine Pastor."

"Did he say anything to you out of the way?"

"No, he was fine."

Pastor had a very serious look on his face. He looked at his watch, "Sit down for a second Angel. He locked the door, "Daughter?"

"Yes Pastor,"

He sighed, "Do you know why I asked you to do hospitality today?"

"No why?"

"Because I feel as though I can trust you to do the right thing."

"What do you mean?"

"You will understand later. Now I know you are a very attractive young woman and the anointing makes you twice as beautiful. You better tell me if someone says something to you out the way. Do you understand me?"

"Yes sir," I replied but I just couldn't tell him about the comment Pastor Strong had made before he left because he had already looked at the man like 'why are you talking to my daughter'. Pastor Peers got up and started towards the door.

"Pastor why would you tell me this or think someone would talk to me in any way?"

"Because I'm a man and I know men, and often times one look at innocent Bathsheba can bring a whirlwind behind it."

"Okay Pastor I understand."

"Okay, but daughter you don't want to ever see that side ever, you want to remain innocent." He grabbed me by the shoulder, "Now let's go and enjoy service."

I exhaled, "Yes sir let's go."

Service was awesome! The Lord really showed himself. There was an awakening in the body that night. I felt as though God had come and broke chains off of lives. I saw people healed and baptized in the Holy Ghost. Before service ended, I had to go back to make sure that Pastor Strong had extra towels, water, and snacks. I sat and waited in the hospitality office. I began to see Pastor Peers, Billy, and Pastor Strong walk towards the Pastor's office.

"Lord tonight was awesome!"

"It was wasn't it?" The Lord replied.

"Yes it was."

"But it's a shame as well."

"Why is it a shame?"

"My word isn't, but the life of that young man is."

"Is that so?"

"Angel, do not get involved with that young man. Listen to your Pastor. He told you everything you needed to know in a couple of sentences."

"Okay, but what's wrong with him?"

"He's living a lie and I know how curious you can be even though I tell you things."

"So what do you mean he lives a lie? And if he lives a lie, how come you use him so mightily?"

"I hurt every time I use him Angel. Sweetheart, people can still work for me and be fired."

"Okay"

"Listen to your Pastor."

There was a knock at the door. It was Pastor Strong smiling. I became very nervous, "Great service!"

"Yeah it was." He took a seat and leaned back in the chair while looking at me with a peculiar gaze. His lips were shifted to the side of his mouth and his eyebrows were raised. "Why are you so stiff girl?"

"No reason."

"Loosen up. I'm only here to tell you thank you for doing such an amazing job making sure I had everything that I needed."

I felt relieved, "You are welcome and it is my job to serve."

He clapped his hands once loudly, "Yes to serve!" My eyes became wider, "Don't worry Angel I'm alright." He reached in his pocket and pulled out a business card, "Here is my card. Now I have a private phone and I took the liberty of writing that number on the back. Whenever you need me or anything you give me a call."

"Goodnight Pastor Strong."

He laid the card on the desk, "If you need anything Angel." He slowly walked out of the door.

I looked at the card lying on the desk, "I'm going to keep your number Pastor Strong and I'm going to pray for you."

The conference had been amazing and went off without a hitch the whole week, but it was now time for Kenya to go. We exchanged numbers so that we could keep in touch with each other and said our goodbyes. I felt refreshed for the next week. It's something about when you have been poured into by the servants of God. It's almost as if you have been watered, received insight about things to come, given direction, and most of all, wisdom.

A few weeks following the conference, even more doors began to open for me. Being at church, preaching the gospel from city to city, state to state, and working seemed to not be enough for me. I was happy with where my anointing had taken me, but at times I would find myself lonely. I didn't understand why all of a sudden I had felt as if I had no friends nor was I dating anyone. I had kept myself so busy that I didn't even realize that I didn't really have personal time with friends and relationships. I would travel with someone that Pastor Peers trusted that I really didn't know and even in that we would never hold a conversation. It almost felt as though they were my body guard whether male or female and they were always way older than I was. Sometimes the pressure that came with ministering would get to me. I constantly would find myself balling up on the floor because there was fire burning on the inside of me. Even though I had Jesus who would always be there and tell me it's okay and comfort me, I began to long for someone to be there to pray with me or hold my hand. One night after I had preached a one weeklong revival, I decided to take myself out to dinner. I walked in the restaurant and sat down and I looked at the menu and I ordered everything I thought would be good to eat no matter the price. I'm pretty sure the people in the restaurant thought I was crazy, but they could not comprehend that this act was as close to spontaneous I had ever gotten in a long while. I sat alone at the table filled with food. I heard Jesus ask, **"You're going to eat all of that?"**

I covered my mouth, "Now Jesus If I sit here and talk to you people are going to think I'm crazy and that I'm talking to myself."

"I understand just talk to me in your mind."

"Okay," in my head I continued, "To answer your question, I just felt the need to do something silly."

"Why?"

"It kind of helps when I don't have anyone to talk to besides you. It's kind of like shopping. Even though you have so many clothes, you always want more."

"So you're not satisfied?"

"No, that is not it." I replied. The whole time I was talking to the Lord a woman at the bar of the restaurant was watching me. I didn't realize I was making faces while I was talking to God without moving my mouth. I then said, "Just a moment Jesus this not working." I then asked the waitress for the check and I left. I then sat in my car and sighed greatly and said, "Now I can talk and no Jesus it's not that I'm not satisfied, it's just that I'm just now realizing that I don't have human friends. I lost contact with Ava over the years and she was my best friend. The only friend I have is you and that's wonderful but I would like to have someone in my life."

"Okay I can understand that."

"I want to even fall in love as well. I have been delighting myself in you and you did say in your word that if I delight myself in you that you will give me the desires of my heart. "

The Lord sighed, **"Yes this is true and it will be done."**

"But when,"

"In time and this season is not the season for that just yet. Now for you to have a friend who is female can be done tomorrow."

"Okay, but why not male?"

"Because you my love are very special to me and when it comes to you and a male, he has to be someone that I approve, not because I have to, but because of what I have placed on the inside of you is very delicate and it cannot be tampered with. Falling in love with the wrong man can tamper with it."

"So in other words," I said, "I may be fifty when I actually date?"

He laughed, **"No you won't be fifty but that wouldn't be such a bad idea."**

"Jesus!"

He laughed again, **"Okay, okay, just don't rush. Love will happen. Allow it to happen and don't force it."**

"Okay I won't."

The next day I decided to go to the park after work to study. I loved the park because it was so large and peaceful. My favorite place to study and meditate was under this large oak tree in the center of the park. While studying I heard someone crying. I looked over to my right and I saw a young lady by the pond sitting on the bench with her hands holding her head. I got up and walked over to her, "Are you okay?"

She then looked at me as she pushed her hair out of her face, "No I'm not okay."

I sat next to her, "I used to cry all the time, I cried so much that I couldn't cry anymore."

She looked at me, "Is that even possible?"

"Yes it is, but the reason as to why I couldn't cry anymore was because I was wounded so bad that I couldn't produce anymore tears for the simple things, nor the things that even made me happy."

"I know you. You're the young lady that everyone talks about who preaches a lot."

"Guilty"

"Evangelist Angel Braveheart,"

I lifted my hands, "Guilty again."

"What are you doing here?"

"Hmmm, I don't know. Maybe I'm here because for some reason I felt the need to be here in the park and now I know why."

She sniffed, "Oh by the way, my name is Carol."

"Nice to meet you Carol, what seems to be the problem? Maybe I can help you."

Carol began to tell me about how she had recently got a divorce and how she never thought that she would have gotten a divorce and that she felt so stupid and should have listened to her Dad when he told her not to marry so young. "I'm twenty eight years old Angel, I wanted to have kids, but I couldn't. My ex-husband became frustrated with the idea of not being a father and often times would say that I was the reason as to why because prior to our marriage, I had an abortion because I wasn't ready to be a mother. He constantly held that over my head. It went from arguing to adultery, to outside child, to divorce." She looked at me, "It's been eight months since our divorce was final and he is engaged to be married again to the woman that had his child."

"I'm sorry to hear all of the pain you have gone through Carol," I grabbed her hand, "But guess what? The story does not end there. Yes, you had a marriage to fail. Now I don't know what that is like and I won't go into detail about that, but I can tell you that at the end of every storm there is always a blessing and Carol this time next year, you won't be the same because I know a man that can take that hurt and turn it into happiness, who will love you and with him there is no divorce and today beloved, we are not going to party over pity. You're going with me and we are going to the mall. We may not have millions, but we are going to act as though we do and whatever we can't buy, we will touch and will have in a short period of time."

She laughed. "Amen." From that moment in the park, Carol and I became really close friends.

A year had past and preaching on the road was now what I had lived and breathed. I traveled so much that I had to quit my job at the dental office. The Lord was truly blessing me. Carol would travel with me as well. Whenever I would feel pressure and the burning on the inside, she would be there praying while holding my hand. Sometimes she didn't understand so she would ask questions.

"We are now in the great state of Georgia," I said as I flopped down on my bed in the hotel room.

"How do you do this Angel?"

"Do what?"

"How do you travel so much and preach and be single?"

"Well Carol….It gets tough sometimes and I don't want to be single, but I know that right now isn't the time for me to be in a relationship."

"Why do you ball up on the floor at night?"

"Because sometimes the word is so strong that when it is about to be released, it feels like my body is on fire."

"Wow! No wonder you're preaching all over. It must feel pretty good to be used by God in such a mighty way."

"It is and I don't mine."

"Angel I want you to know that I really appreciate all that you have done for me as a friend."

"Awe girl, you're welcome. I'm thankful to God for you as well. It did get a little lonely not having a friend to talk to."

"Trust me Angel, I know that feeling,"

"Alright Carol, I'm going to get some rest before tonight's service and if the Pastor of the church calls, tell him we are here and to give you all the information we need. Wake me up two hours before six."

"Okay get some rest."

After so many months of travel and preaching even the friendship with Carol wasn't enough, I finally told God that I was not satisfied and that I wanted to be in love. I wanted a husband. I began to wrestle with God even though I knew it was too soon. I really believed that I was ready and that it was time. A year and six months had past but Jesus would not budge so I decided to take matters into my own hands.

I remembered that I had Pastor Strong's number and without thinking about anything that the Lord had previously told me I called him.

"You've reached Pastor Jeremy Strong," he said after answering the phone.

"Hi this Angel I don't know if…"

"Angel, I remember you very well! I was hoping that you called. I was just thinking of you a couple of months ago. You were…"

"Yes," I was…"

It's been a while and I have been hearing some great things about you,"

"Well praise the Lord," I said.

"Yeah, praise him girl. So you're enjoying the preaching life?"

"I am. I'm really so thankful to God and blessed."

"That is a blessing. So tell me Angel, what will you be doing around the second week in September?"

"Well, I will have to see because I am booked up until next year."

"Girl, go on with your bad self."

"No, go Jesus because I have nothing to do with that. Why do you ask?"

"Because I would love it if I could have you out here to my church and preach for me."

"Well I will have to check my calendar and speak with my Pastor, but we will see what happens."

"You better make time for me."

"Like I said I will check my schedule."

"So are you dating anyone Angel?"

"No, I'm not."

He chuckled. "Well that's what I was hoping you would say."

I laughed. "And why is that?"

"Because I want to be the one who gets that opportunity."

"Pastor Strong you just don't know when to quit."

"Angel when a man meets a woman like you. You know he is always going to come hard because you're everything that he could ever imagine: young, beautiful, intelligent, and an anointed a woman of God. Mmmm, mmmh, mmh. That is priceless and hard to find."

"Well you know Pastor, there are a lot of those women out there, but often they are looked over, hurt, and broken all because of men like you."

"Men like me?"

"Yes I'm sure you have broken hearts and hurt a couple of women."

"Oh Angel, everyone has done that and I won't be the first nor the last."

"Hmm I see."

"Woman, I am a lover not a fighter. Would you like for me to prove that to you?"

"No, prove that to God."

"Okay, okay Ms. Angel, I see that you are one tough cookie, and I don't blame you at all but all I have is one thing to say to you."

"What's that?"

Pastor Strong became silent for a split moment, "You will fall in love with me."

"Is that right?"

"That will be right."

We talked on the phone for hours and found ourselves lost in conversation. It was so refreshing to talk to a man that had seen a lot and that was knowledgeable of the scripture. I heard the Lords voice, **"Tell him goodnight Angel."**

I looked up towards the heavens and moved my lips saying one sec please.

"We have to talk Angel."

I sighed. "Pastor Strong can we continue this conversation some other time. I have to go to a meeting."

"Of course and we said our goodbyes.

I slowly laid my cell on the table and looked up. "Yes Lord."

The Lord sighed and I felt a brush of wind blow pass me that made the hairs on my arms stand at attention. **"Angel, what did I tell you about this man?"**

"But Jesus"

"Angel," he thundered, **"He is no good for you. He's not ready for what you are ready for."**

"But I was just talking to him,"

"No Angel you were lusting."

"Jesus I'm tired of being alone. I know that you are here and I love that so much but I want someone to fall in love with and to laugh with."

"Angel, I know and I understand, but this man will only lead you down a path that you are not ready for."

"So you think I can't handle the things that life has to bring?"

"No, I created you. I know you can handle the things that life throws at you, but why stand in the mist of those things when you can bypass them?"

"Okay Jesus, how about this, how about I date him and if I see that things are going south, I will end it."

 "Angel"

"I just want to fall in love and maybe he will change. Even you looked upon Adam and saw that he was lonely and gave him a wife, so what about me?"

"Angel, Okay I warned you. It's your choice. Just know that I love you and I will always be with you."

"I love you to Lord and thank you, maybe something good will come out of this."

"I love you Angel," His voice faded away.

Months passed by and Pastor Strong and I was now official. He would call me five times a day and also send me flowers, cards, and gifts. We would have lunch out of state and enjoy the city. It was everything that I had dreamed about. I thought I was the luckiest woman in the world. One day he had closed an entire restaurant just for us. When we finished the best meal that I have ever tasted, he looked up at me with his dark brown eyes, "Angel I have never been happier in my whole life, and I thank God for you. You are indeed an Angel. I just have one question."

"What is that?"

"Will you be my Queen?"

I smiled, "And what is that to you?"

"Angel, how would you like to be the first lady of fifteen thousand members?"

"Wow that is a lot to take on."

"Yes it is Angel; do you remember the Story of Ruth and Boaz?"

"I do."

"Well, before Ruth married Boaz, he gave her a part of the field, but when he married her, she received the whole field."

"Okay"

"I will give you everything if you say yes to being my Queen."

I looked at him while slowly looking up and down thinking. I got up and slowly walked over to the other side of the dinner table where Pastor Strong was sitting and looked him in the eyes, "Pastor Strong I don't want anything else but you, your love, your support and your honesty. I'll be your Queen only if you give me just that."

Pastor Strong looked at me with water in his eyes and a big smile, "I can. I definitely can do that Angel." He stood up and hugged me gently followed by a kiss on the cheek.

We spent so much time together and after eight months of dating things began to take a turn in our relationship. I would travel so much that he began to get irritated because I would have so many things to do. One night in particular was marked by something that I didn't see coming.

Bam! Bam! Bam! "Angel!"

Pastor Strong was beating on my hotel door.

I didn't expect him to be in the same place that I was in. I opened the door, "What is it?"

As he walked in he started looking around the room. "Angel are you sleeping with someone?"

I was completely in shock. "Wow, wait a minute, hello how are you? That would be nice to ask." He was furious. He threw the chair across the room that was at the desk. "Are you okay? What is wrong with you?"

"Angel I received a call that there was a young man taking you to your room last night."

"Oh yeah, the driver from the church, he was making sure I made it here safely because my friend could not come with me."

"Angel, why didn't you tell me you were coming here alone?"

"Why didn't you tell me that you had someone spying on me?" I placed my hand over my forehead, "Okay, this is crazy. You know I'm not sleeping with anyone. Heck I'm not even sleeping with you!"

He sat down on the bed, "I know you are a good woman. I just fear losing you sometimes. I know I can make a lot of mistakes. I just don't want us to be one of those mistakes."

I rolled my eyes, "Save it okay. I'm not going anywhere and you can tell your spies to stop watching me."

He burst into laughter as though what I said was funny, "I love you Angel."

I folded my arms together as my leg bounced "And...."

"And I will tell my spies to lay off my girl."

"Thank you, I would appreciate that."

Pastor Strong grabbed my face and began to kiss me. I pushed him away, "What are you doing?"

"Angel it's been eight months."

"I know and I want to wait until we are married."

"Listen Angel, I believe in that too but I have needs. I'm a man..."

"Well I'm not ready."

"But I thought you were my Queen?"

"I am."

"Angel, everyone knows that we are together."

"Yes, I know."

"You're going to be my First Lady."

"That doesn't move me."

"So, let's just have our night. I love you Angel, you're mine."

"I love you too but…"

"No buts Angel." He began to kiss me and caress me.

The next morning as I was waking up, I saw Pastor Strong getting dressed.

"Where are you going? I asked.

"Oh I have to fly back in and handle some business."

"Okay I better be getting going myself."

"Last night was amazing Angel."

"Oh was it?"

"Yes it was."

I got up and walked into the bathroom. He yelled, "I have something for you when you come out Angel, but I have to go. Enjoy it okay!"

"Okay, I will, thank you baby!"

"No problem, love you!"

After I got out of the shower and got ready to go, I noticed ten one hundred dollar bills on the night stand. I thought to myself, "I know he just did not leave me no money on this night stand like I was a hooker." I grabbed my cell and called him. He answered, "Mr. Strong, why did you leave money on my dresser like I was a hooker?"

He laughed, "It wasn't a statement Angel."

"It was laying there as though it was a natural thing for you."

He laughed again, "Baby I just thought that you might want to enjoy yourself once you got back home. No biggie, I know you are not a hooker…boy women will put thought into everything a man does."

"Women?"

"You know what I mean baby," he quickly responded.

"Okay, I was just calling to see."

"Angel enjoy yourself please on me."

"I will," I quickly hung up the phone.

"Lord," I said while looking towards the heavens, "Please forgive me. I fornicated last night and it wasn't something I wanted to do. But I think I did it because I think I am falling in love with this man. I truly believed that he has changed. Please forgive me and I love you so much."

After praying that prayer over fifty times, I realized that I was in with Pastor Strong really deep. It was now a year and seven months into our relationship. He stopped talking about commitment and even if someone asked, he would change the subject. I would travel and preach the Gospel, but I felt as though I was living a lie. I was sleeping with a man that was not my husband. People looked at us and even though they didn't say it, they knew what was going on between us. I noticed that when I preached there was no power behind it at all, no matter how hard I preached. Pastor Strong and I began to go back and forth arguing and even cursing one another. At times I would feel so alone that I would lie on my bathroom floor and cry. I could hear God's warning over and over in my head but I could not believe it because I just knew that if I continued to be the woman that he wanted, he would change his mind and commit to me. There would be women calling his phone that I didn't know and the five times a day of calling turned into once a day or maybe once every other week. But I still believed that he was going to change as long as I remained that woman that he wanted.

"Oh my Lord Angel, it's a plus sign!" Carol said while holding the pregnancy test that I had just taken.

"Are you serious? This can't be right, let me try another one because sometimes they could be wrong." I went through ten more of the pregnancy tests and all of them were positive. I broke down right in front of Carol and I could hardly catch my breath, "I don't think I can do this. Carol, I can't do this, I can't, not anymore."

"Do what Angel? It'll be okay, I know it will."

"No it won't," I said, "I can't believe this. We were careful Carol we made sure. He's not going to believe me at all."

"He has no choice or else he can take a blood test,"

"What about the ministry Carol and what about the people?"

Carol became angry, "What about them! You have a child inside of you. Forget people right now, you have been given something that I will never experience and you are worried about people!"

"You don't understand. My life is over, everything that I worked hard for."

"Angel! Snap out of it okay, you will be alright. Having sex was the mistake, not the child, always remember that God knows best."

That whole week I did not hear from Pastor Strong nor did I care. I didn't even want to hear his voice, nor the lecture behind it. All I could think about was the fact that I had ten more revivals coming up and the rest I had to cancel because by that time I would be huge.

While laying on my bed in my room I heard Jesus call,

"Angel."

"Yes Lord."

"I'm here,"

I began to cry, "How, why?"

"Now sweetheart, this may look like the end to you but it is actually the beginning."

"I'm pregnant, how could that be?"

"Angel, you did not stop when things were going south and you said you would. But you were right about one thing you said."

"And what was that?"

"You said that who knows something good may come out of it. Angel, this is good and the best part is that it is not about you."

"He's not going to believe me, Jesus,"

"But I do, I love you."

"What about ministry?"

"Angel this is ministry,"

"But how? I don't understand."

"You will, I promise."

Three weeks later, I received a phone call from Pastor Strong, "Hey baby what's going on?"

"A lot," I answered.

He chuckled, "I'm so sorry I haven't called. I have been so busy with the church and preaching and meetings."

"Okay that's wonderful."

"Baby you sound a little upset, are you ready to see me?"

"As a matter of fact, I am."

"Okay how about we fly out to an island and relax and get our feet wet."

"No, I'm good. I would rather come to your home instead."

"You don't want to go anywhere else?"

"No, I would rather come see you at your place."

"Okay well check your email in about two hours for your ticket and come on out and I'm all yours."

"Okay, I will."

I could not wait until the next morning to catch the early flight that Pastor Strong had scheduled for me. The plane ride gave me a lot of time to think about how I was going to tell Pastor Strong that I was pregnant. For about fifteen minutes I convinced myself that things may actually go swell. I was imagining that he would pick me up in his arms and say with a loud voice, 'marry me!' just as every other woman would imagine the father of their unborn child would say. I said to myself, 'yeah right' and began to prepare my heart for the worse.

"There's my baby," Pastor Strong said waiting for me at baggage claim.

"I looked at him in frustration, "Hello, how are you?"

He hugged me, "I'm so happy right now Angel."

"Huh, I bet, it would have been nice to receive flowers today Pastor Strong."

He looked at me while holding my shoulders, "Oh so my presence isn't enough?"

"No actually it's not."

He laughed, "I see someone is in a bad mood today, so before we start going south let me just tell you how much I missed you."

While getting into the limo he began to go on and on about how much he missed me and how God had gotten on to him about neglecting me for the past few weeks and how he knows that he will never find another woman like me. I could not take it anymore I yelled, "I'm pregnant!"

Pastor Strong looked at me as if he was getting choked, "What?"

I said softly, "I'm pregnant."

"How did this happen?" he asked.

"You're really asking me that question?"

"Yes, because Angel, I have not been with you in almost a month."

"Well I am more than a month!"

"Angel, this baby couldn't possibly be mine."

"Well whose is it then if it's not yours?"

"I don't know Angel that is between you and God."

I looked at him with anger in my eyes, "Are you hearing yourself? You know that I have not been with anyone else, you know this!"

"Angel I wasn't able to have kids with my ex wife what makes you think that I can have kids with you?"

"Are you fixed?"

"No."

"Do you have a low sperm count?"

"No,"

"Then what makes you think that you could not have gotten me pregnant?"

"But Angel, I mean... I made sure that this would not happen. I know my body and I didn't get you pregnant. You better go and try and call the knuckle head that got you knocked up because I'm not the one."

"Oh okay, you want me to call him huh." I reached into my purse and held up my phone, "Okay, let me see hmmm...hmmm." I called Pastor Strong's number privately, "Okay, let me see will he answer."

Pastor Strong's phone began to ring as he told me hold on for a sec," Hello?"

"I'm glad you answered," I said, "I had to call you and let you know I'm pregnant with your child."

"Angel that is not funny."

"You told me to call him!"

"See Angel, that's why I wasn't going to even talk to you anymore, you're nothing but trouble!"

"Trouble!"

"Yeah, trouble, you women preachers make me sick!"

"Oh really?"

"Yeah, really, y'all always talking about how good God is; and then you open up your legs to every man that says 'you can preach' or invites you to their church!"

I looked at him, "You are so wrong!"

"Oh Angel I'm not done. You just want me because I have preached all over this country and got all of this fame and all of the lights are on me. Heck, I was even humble enough to even share it with you, but I see you have messed that up. You thought you were something huh? But I could see right through your cheap make-up that you were just like all of the rest of the women out there. Angel you think that you will get a little fame because you're pregnant? I'm going to let you have it baby, be my guest, enjoy yourself, I have been through a divorce and slept with countless of women and guess what, I'm still better than you on any given day! You're stupid and pathetic, and I have no sympathy for women like you or any woman at all that calls themselves a preacher." Water was flowing from my eyes as he proceeded, "You are nothing and you will never be anything. Oh and guess who will have to put the mic down and guess who will still travel the world with a mic in their hands? Hmmm… you don't know. Well I can tell you that it won't be you! Matter of fact you are not even worthy to ride in the back of my limo! Driver! Please pull over!"

I began to cry hysterically, "How could you do this to me?"

"Angel, get out of my car."

"We're on the side of a freeway!"

"Didn't I say that you are not worthy to be in my limo? Get out or I will throw you and that bastard child out of my limo!"

I suddenly heard Jesus, **"Angel hold your head up and don't say a word and get out of the car. I'm here."**

I looked at Pastor Strong and got out of the limo.

The limo spun off. I fell to the ground, "Why didn't I listen to you, Father! I'm so sorry, I'm so sorry, please forgive me and help me, please, because I'm about to lose my mind, I can't breathe! Oh God have mercy! I don't know who I am anymore! What am I going to do? I have nothing."

"Get up! You listen to me, the best thing you ever did was get out of that limo because that young man is headed for a storm that I could not let you enter. You will be okay."

"But he denied our child and called him a bastard."

"Angel, am I not the Father of all Fathers?"

"Yes, you are."

"Then as long as that child lives, there will never be a Fatherless day for that child that you carry in your womb."

"But what about ministry?"

"Angel, this is ministry!"

"I can't see it, Lord; I've screwed up so much. I just wanted to be happy Lord, I just…"

"Angel, I don't care about the times you have messed up. I'm only concerned with right now. And right now, I'm sending you a cab."

Right after the Lord spoke, a cab driver pulled up right beside me on the freeway, "You need a ride Miss?"

I got up and nodded, "Yeah I do."

I got into the cab. I looked and felt awful. The cab driver asked, "So where am I taking you?"

I sighed. "The airport,"

"Are you okay Miss?"

I didn't respond. He looked at me through his rear view mirror, "Well ma'am I don't know what you are or going through, but God will definitely take care of it."

I looked up at him, "Thank you sir."

When we arrived at the airport, the cab driver came around to open my door and reached in his pocket, "I know this may sound crazy Miss, but before I came to work today, the Lord said to give a woman eight hundred dollars. I said to myself that yeah I'm going to see a lot of women today, and to tell you the truth miss, I have been at work all day and my only riders have been men. I don't know why I have to give it to you, but I know that I must be obedient and I know that you must be one special young lady in the eyes of the Lord."

I looked at him as I got out of the car and I gave him a big hug, "It's for my plane ticket home! Thank you for being obedient and you will be blessed tremendously!"

"God bless you ma'am and I pray for you to have safe travels. But before you go, I have one question."

"What's that?"

"What were you going to do had I not been obedient?"

I slowly looked at him, and looked up towards the sky, "Pray." We both went our separate ways.

Chapter Six

"Compassion"

It had now come the time to where I had to preach at my last revival for the year. I was four months pregnant and no one knew but my mom and Carol. That was a night that I will never forget, even though I felt liked Joseph, 'blessed but in a mess'. I preached my heart out as though it was my last time. I didn't hear anything from Pastor Strong and I didn't even care anymore. I went back to my old job at the dentist office and I even got a place of my own that was far from the city of Belle Mede. After that night, I isolated myself in my small apartment. I didn't talk to anyone but my mother and God. I didn't even talk to the people at work. I felt as though I had nothing to say. I would cry myself to sleep every night while holding my pillows tight. I found myself thinking suicidal thoughts again, but they did not prevail. Angels would watch me as I slept at night and even take me to the bathroom. The Lord made sure that I was taken care of. In the morning, they would each wake me up with a word imprinted on the front of their belts that wrapped around their robes. Sometimes it would be 'happy' and other times, 'loved' or 'patience'. For some reason, the word was the only thing that always stood out. I took it as the Lord was just trying to make me feel a lot better than I was feeling.

"Angel," the Lord said, **"Get up!"**

I spoke as still lie in bed, "Lord why? I feel awful today; can't I just lay here for a few more minutes?"

"No, get up and pray Angel."

I let out a big sigh and got up from my bed and prayed. After praying I had to ask, "Lord, why do you wake me up to pray? And why do you still love me? I'm sure everyone else will shun me, why not you?"

"Angel I wake you up to pray because the prayer of the righteous avails much. And I am not like anyone that you have ever met."

I looked up towards the heavens, "You think I'm righteous? I'm giving birth to a child and I am not married."

"By which you have been forgiven, Angel you are not just praying for right now, but for things to come. That child that you carry in your womb will be blessed and you both will never have to worry about

anything. My love for you runs deep and if I were to tell you why I love you so, it would take eternity. I would begin even before you were placed in your mother's womb and I would never finish the reason from there. I want you to be happy because you are loved and be patient because there is a blessing behind what you are going through."

"The words the Angels have on their belts every morning. Thank you so much for loving me and being here for me Jesus, I love you so much."

Time passed and I was now eight months pregnant with a baby boy. I had been receiving phone calls from Pastor Peers and his wife throughout my pregnancy, but I never responded because I was ashamed. Even though they did not know, I was not ready to tell them early on in my pregnancy. I felt as though since it was almost time for the arrival of my son that I should call and tell them.

"Hello," Lady Peers answered the phone.

"Hey Lady, how are you?"

"Angel! Is that you?"

"Yes ma'am it is I, are you busy?"

"I'm never too busy for you Angel. What's going on, we haven't heard from you or seen you in I don't know, a year, where are you?"

"I'm about thirty minutes away and I am about to have a son."

"Angel, shut up!"

"Yes, I'm only a few weeks away from being a mother."

"Well did you get married Angel?"

"No, I didn't get married."

"Oh Angel"

"But I'm okay, and all I ask is for your prayers."

"Angel, I will always be here if you need me and I am going to be praying for you and that baby. If you need me just call me."

"Okay, tell Pastor Peers hello!"

"I sure will,"

"Okay, have a blessed day Lady Peers,"

"You too Angel Talk to you soon," I then hung up my phone

When I turned thirty eight weeks I decided to stay with my mom until my son's arrival. She was so wonderful and she made sure that I was comfortable.

"Come on Angel you can do it. Give me a big push, just one big one!" The Doctor yelled at me. I pushed harder than ever before and out came my son, Micah Braveheart. That was the most amazing day of my life. I was finally a mother. I took one look at my little prince and fell in love with him. He was so beautiful. He was born seven pounds, ten point three ounces, twenty inches long, and healthy. He had all of my features from my dark skin tone to my dark brown eyes and black curly hair. I was so happy to finally see his face after all those months of carrying him. My life had started a new journey all over again. After staying in the hospital for two days, my mom drove us back to her house. Family was coming from everywhere just to see Micah. Everyone was so excited and I was so glad that no one had asked me who his father was and I hated to think about it. I was so glad that my Aunt Missy had moved because had she been there, that question would have been asked and she would have spoiled everyone's day. The next two weeks were tough, and had I not had my mom, I would not have known what to do. I realized that having a child takes two because you would have to be supermom to take on this all by yourself without the assistance of anyone. From waking up in the middle of the night to changing diapers, there were so many sleepless nights. I was so busy with Micah that I didn't realize that I was not eating or keeping myself up. I see why the Lord did what he did one night.

"**Angel,**" the Lord said.

"Yes Lord."

"**Get some rest.**"

"What about the baby? He's going to wake up soon."

"**No he won't Angel. He's going to sleep a little longer tonight.**"

"Okay, but what if…"

"**Angel, you let me worry about him. You get some rest.**"

I looked at Micah and looked up towards the Lord, "Okay I trust you and thank you." I quickly fell asleep. I had the best sleep ever. Micah really did sleep throughout the night, and this wasn't supposed to happen until his third month. Jesus is awesome. He allowed my child to carry out this routine until I was well rested every night up until he was six months old. One night as I was sitting on my bed in my old room, I couldn't help but get teary eyed looking at my son. I thought about what I could do to make his life easier. I didn't want him to go through any of the things that I had gone through financially or emotionally. I felt as though my preaching career was over all because of my situation. Nobody cared to even listen to anything I had to say anymore. I looked towards the Lord and said with tears in my eyes, "What am I going to do Jesus? I have a son. My job doesn't pay much. I have some college education, but I didn't finish. People won't allow me to speak in their church anymore as their comments about my situation now are haunting me. It hurts because they don't understand and the money that I saved is leaving quickly. I'm running out of options. What am I going to do?"

"Angel, first you are going to wipe the tears from your eyes; second, we are not going to talk about people; and third, you are not running out of money because you have me. I'll give you everything you need, just trust me."

"Okay, I trust you. It's all you this time and not me. Do whatever you please Lord and I will follow you."

"Weeping may endure for a night Angel, but joy, joy will come in the morning."

Once Micah was seven months old, I had to take him to Pastor Davis and give him back to the Lord. It felt strange to walk into the church after so many years. People were looking and whispering. I heard one lady say, "I knew it. Couldn't fool me," as I was going to the restroom after service. I walked in and locked the door and cried. People can be so cruel.

I heard my mom knock on the door, "Angel."

I sniffed, "I'll be out in a second."

"Okay, but Micah is getting cranky and I'm ready to go."

"I'm coming,"

I opened the door, "You okay Angel?"

"I'm alright." I grabbed my son and we left.

While Micah was sleeping I talked to the Lord. "Okay Jesus, you are right. I'm not going to cry anymore or feel bad because my son is a blessing to me and I'm not going to do it my way anymore. I'm going to do it your way. So tell me, give me steps to help me. You are all I have and I am fully leaning and depending on you to help me. You tell me and I'll do it."

"Okay Angel, go back to school and finish your degree."

"Huh? How will I....?" I stopped myself, "Yes, sir. I'll go back to school and finish my degree in Biology." I looked up again, "Okay school, got it, what else?"

"Be patient."

"Okay, but what about…"

"Be patient, pray, study your bible,"

"That's it?"

"Yes Angel that's it."

After the Lord told me what to do, I became very frustrated because I was so used to doing what I wanted to do and making things my own. However, because he was leading me, I never knew what to expect. I mean at least when I did things, I could think about what to expect, but this was totally different. I gave him full and total control and even though I trusted him completely, I was nervous because I never knew what to expect.

The next Sunday I decided to let Micah go to church with my mom because I wanted to go to the church to hear Pastor Peers and see him and his wife. Church was amazing there as usual and when it was over, I decided to go to Pastor Peer's office. I knocked on the door and a young lady came out, "Hey!" She greeted.

"Hello is the Lady and Pastor in?" I asked.

"Yes go right in. "

I walked in smiling, "Hey!"

"Angel!" Pastor Peers yelled.

"Hello Pastor, how are you?"

He hugged me, "I'm wonderful, how have you been and how is the baby?"

"I'm great and he is fine. He's with my mom."

"Well you should have brought him to see us."

"Yeah, I know." I realized that the whole time Lady Peers didn't say anything. She just sat there with her arms folded and legs crossed. I looked over towards her, "Hey Lady, how are you?"

"I'm good Angel. It's good to see you."

I looked around, "Did I come at a bad time?"

"Oh no," Pastor said, "You are good. We are glad you are here."

"Okay well I better get going, I got to pick up the baby."

"Oh no, will you be back this week?" Pastor Peers asked.

"Sure I will."

"Great, because I have some wonderful things coming up and I want you to be a part of it Angel.

"Okay sure, I will definitely be back." Pastor Peers walked over and grabbed my shoulder and looked in my eyes.

"Angel, don't worry, we're going to help you get back to where you need to be."

"Great…well I guess I'll see you guys next week."

Pastor Peers smiled, but Lady Peers continued to just sit there. I slowly turned to walk out the door.

As walked out the door, the young lady that had left was walking back in the Pastor Study.

Suddenly I had the urge to use the restroom so I turned around and walked back that way towards the restroom. As I was getting closer to the door, I heard Lady Peers whispering to the young lady, "How did she get in here?"

The young lady said, "I let her in."

Lady Peers whispered in anger, "I don't want that whore in this office."

"I'm sorry," the girl exclaimed, "She's one of the ministers."

Lady Peers affirmed, "I don't care if she wants to talk to the Pastor, you make sure you consult me first."

I placed my hands over my mouth because I could not believe that the same woman that shouts throughout church and said that she would be there for me and that she would pray for me would say this about me. I forgot about the restroom and went home.

At home, I paced the floor with Micah in my arms, "Lord why do people think they know me? I may have had a baby, but I'm not a whore! All I did was have a baby without having a ring on my finger and this is how people label me? She's worried about me being a whore, she better be worried about the ones around her being one!"

"Angel!" the Lord thundered, **"Put Micah down."** I placed Micah in his swing. **"What she said was wrong Angel, and I know that it made you upset, but don't speak of that around Micah. Don't ever talk like that around him. You shouldn't want to say that at all. Yes she was wrong and threw a stone, but you should not throw them back even when they can't see them nor when they can."**

"I'm not going to cry anymore Lord, but that did hurt me."

"I know it did, but it's okay, you will be okay."

After hearing the things people had to say about me, I decided not to go to church anymore, I didn't want to be near church folk. I told the Lord that I didn't want to go back to church because all people do is make you feel bad when you go. I told him that I would have church at home instead and I did. Me and Micah, we had church at home. In the process of having church at home, I had also enrolled back in school to finish my Biology degree. Several months had gone by and I seemed to be doing quite well. Micah was getting bigger each day and he had begun to talk a little. He would say 'mama', 'hi', and 'bye' and it was so beautiful watching him grow up. After Micah's first birthday, I decided to go into the city to get me some new clothes because my old ones did not fit anymore. I walked into a men and women clothing store and I began to look around. I immediately heard a familiar voice. I looked up and it was my dad. I walked quickly over shouting, "Dad!"

He curiously looked at me for a long time, "Angel."

I hugged him so tight, "Daddy where have you been! I have missed you so much. I have been praying for you, I have so much to tell you!"

He pushed me back and looked at the woman standing next to him and looked back at me, "Angel it's good to see you too, look at you you're a grown woman now!"

"Yep", "You're a Granddad now too."

He looked at me once again after looking at the woman. "Angel this is my wife Gloria."

I shook her hand, "Hi Gloria, nice to meet you."

He looked down at the floor and wiped his forehead, "I see your mother never told you huh?"

I looked at him strange, "Told me what?"

He sighed, "Angel, I'm not your Father."

At that moment my heart sunk into my back. I blinked twice slowly. I was so hurt that I couldn't speak briefly. I said slowly and softly, "What did you just say?"

He grabbed me and hugged me, "Angel there has not been a day that went by that I have not thought of you and I'm sorry sweetheart, but I'm not your Father. I can't believe your Mother has not told you after all these years, I'm sorry."

I felt myself getting sick I pushed him away, "I ran to the restroom and I threw up. I just sat in the restroom, I tried to cry, but I couldn't get any tears to fall from my eyes. I got up and left the store and I went straight to my Mom's.

While I drove home, I thought about all the things Mom would tell me and how she would call that man my Dad and how I never understood why he left me. But, it was because he was never was my Dad to began with. The day the man left, he was telling my mom the truth when he told her "that is your daughter". As I walked into my mom's house, she yelled to me while holding Micah's hand, "Angel, look he is walking!" I interrupted,

"Why didn't you tell me John wasn't my real Father?"

My mom looked at me her eyes became bigger, "Who told you that?"

I replied sternly, "Answer my question!" "Why didn't you tell me that John was not my Father?

"He is your Father Angel."

"Stop It Mom!" I just saw the man and he told me that he was not my Dad. I was so happy to finally see him after all these years and he tells me that he cannot believe that after all these years you never told me that. I looked like a fool! And you still sit there and lie in my face. Tell me the truth Mom, is John my Dad or not?!" I want to hear it from you!

"Okay! Okay Angel, John is not your Father."

I became so angry with my mom that I grabbed Micah and his things, "How could you Mom? I thought he didn't love me? I thought that he hated us, but all this time he just hated you!" I grabbed our things and left.

My Mom must have called me over thirty times that night, but I didn't answer nor did I care at that time. I didn't even know who my Father was.

I sighed. "Lord, why didn't you tell me John wasn't my Father?"

"I did, who you think placed him in your path?"

"Why now and not years ago?"

"Because you weren't ready and you needed your Mom. Had you found out then, you would have not spoken to her and shut her out of your life."

"Lord, I can't even cry about it you know,"

"Angel just listen to what your mother has to say."

"I can't. I don't what to talk to her. She's a liar!"

"Angel I know you are hurt, but you only have one Mother. Go to her and talk to her."

"Lord I can't."

After a month of not speaking with my Mother, I decided to go by her house and see her. I wanted to know the truth so I took the time to prepare myself for what she was about to tell me.

"Aww hey! There is my handsome grandbaby?" She yelled.

"Yeah," I said while guiding Micah by the hands towards her.

She began to talk to Micah and play with him. I became anxious, "Okay Mom, let's talk, what happened between you and John? And who is my real Dad?"

My mom took a deep breath, "Okay, after twelve years of marriage, John and I began to get a little rocky due to people in the community telling him that you were not his child. I thought that it was over once you were born, but his family would not let it go. It continued after you turned eight. I guess he just got tired and he decided to find out the truth. Angel do you remember him taking you to his cousin Shelia, the doctor?"

I sighed, "Vaguely."

"Well, he took you to her to get DNA results behind my back and when the results came back, you were not his daughter."

"So you cheated on John?"

"Yes Angel I did, but he is no saint either you know, that was the reason why I cheated. John has a son that's a lot older than you. He conceived him a month after we were married."

"Wow, so who is my Father?"

"Are you sure you want to know?"

"Yes Mom, I want to know."

She hesitated and looked at me, "Pastor James Peers."

"No Mom!"

"Yes Angel and I have the proof." My mom grabbed a box from underneath the table and showed me the paternity results along with check receipts. She looked at me ashamed and proceeded, "He and Pastor Davis are very close. I thought that Pastor Davis was going to tell you and after he sent you to that church, I had to confront him about it, but your Dad wanted you to be close to him. I couldn't get a chance to speak with him because it would hurt his wife."

"Mom, she doesn't know?"

My Mom looked at me with water in her eyes and guilt in her heart, "No Angel she doesn't know."

I grabbed my Mom as she began to cry, "I'm so sorry Angel, I'm so sorry."

I patted her on the back, "It's okay, Mama it's okay. People make mistakes, it's okay."

"My mom wiped her eyes, "But you can't say anything about this Angel."

"Why not?"

"Angel please I have gone through enough, we have kept this silent for twenty seven years."

"Okay Mom, I won't say anything, but I will let him know that I know."

"How will you do that?"

"I'll figure something out, but I won't tell anyone."

After hearing the truth about who my Dad was, I was relieved. No wonder he was so nice to me, I thought, and no wonder he didn't shun me like everyone else. My dad was one of the most well known Pastors in the world and he had a secret that no one knew. It was the story of my life all over again with my son. I prayed that this curse would be broken with him. I spent hours in prayer and anointed Micah's head with oil and prayed over him and his life. Then something unusual happened to me. I saw a vision that his life was not going to be like any of ours and that the curse was broken. I had never had a vision before and it was quite refreshing to see.

After finding out that Pastor Peers was my Dad, I went online and read about him, to try and get to know a little bit more about him. I realized that I didn't even really know him and that I was fatherless. I felt bad for myself, but it hit me. No, Pastor Peers was not my Father either, because a Father is there for their children no matter what. A Father guides their children and corrects them when they are wrong. A Father is patient and loving, he's always there. I looked up towards heaven and said, "Lord that is what you have been to me, a Father! You never left me. You have always been there for me no matter what, and from this day forward, you're my Father. You deserve the title and so much more! And I honor you for that! I praise you for that! Because you are one awesome Father!"

I heard the Lord, **"Angel I was your Father before you were born and will gladly continue from this day forth and throughout eternity."**

I looked up slowly towards the heavens and smiled, "I love you so much Father."

Chapter Seven

"Joy"

"Awe Baby I'm so proud of you!" My mother yelled out to me while I began to take a picture with Micah. It was my graduation day at Bella Mede University and I was so excited. I finally did it! I was now twenty nine years old and Micah was three. Life was different and now it was even better than ever. I had just got a job at the hospital to work in the lab which was crazy favor, and my very own home. I owed it to no one but my Father in heaven. Even though I hadn't been to a church house in three years, I still held on to what I had told the Lord. That I would not stop and that church would be in my home. And he still remained faithful to me.

"Okay," Carol said, "Just one more picture!"

Carol had gotten remarried and not only that, but they were also expecting their first child that fall. I was so happy for her. It felt good but for some reason I could feel my spirit tossing and turning on the inside of me.

"Angel," Carol said, "I just want to let you know as a friend that I am so proud of you and I pray that the Lord continues to bless you more and more!"

"Thank you so much Carol and same to you. I can't wait to teach that little girl everything her Auntie knows."

"So what's next?" Carol asked.

"I don't know. You know I'm just allowing God to do whatever he wants to do in my life right now."

"Well…. I know that you haven't dated in years."

"Oh Lord, Carol you know I'm not thinking about dating."

"I know Angel, but hear me out, Anthony and I have someone we would like for you to meet."

I moped, "Oh Lord I don't know Carol."

"Come on Angel, you could use some male interaction."

"Carol, okay, but he better be a good one. What are his credentials?"

"Great! Okay, he's your age. He and Anthony just became friends. He is a Pastor."

"Oh Lord! Carol!"

"Angel! Stop it! Now listen, he's never been married. He has no children and he is a Professor at Western University."

"Really? Hmmm, I used to go there."

"Well good, you two would have something to talk about. Now this is a blind date. Anthony has told him about you, but he didn't tell him your name."

"Oh Lord Carol,"

"So I cannot tell you his."

"So how are we supposed to know each other?"

"You let me and Anthony worry about that, you just say you will go out with him."

"I don't know Carol,"

"Oh, come on Angel!"

"Okay I'll go if it makes you feel better."

"Yes, that's my girl!" Carol was so happy to be hooking me up with someone. "Okay Angel I'll let you know everything this Friday because he is coming down."

"Carol!"

"Hey you can thank me later. Just be ready at seven and I'll give you the details then."

I could not believe Carol had really just set me up with someone. That night at home I had to talk to my Father about it.

"Father, I don't know about this blind date thing. I have not been successful when it comes to men, you know that."

"But Angel, you are ready now."

"What?! Did you just say that?!"

The Lord laughed, **"Yes, it's time."**

"Well, can you give me any hints of who this may be?"

"Sorry no can do, but I will say this: I trust him with you."

I laughed. "Wow, now I know something is up. You're letting me date a guy you approve of. Wow, he must be wonderful… I bet he's not cute!"

"Angel!"

"Okay, okay I'm sorry, but Father I want to stay a little girl and not think about relationships and stuff."

"And that is how I know you are ready. You will be glad you went, I promise."

After that conversation with my Father, I thought that this blind date thing could be really cool. Besides, the way my life had begun to blossom it must have been my season to be happy.

Friday came so fast. My heart was pounding and I did not know what to wear. I just felt like nothing was perfect, even Micah frowned at a couple of my outfits. I then received a call from Carol.

"Hey Girl are you ready?"

"Yeah I guess," I groaned.

"Okay great!" I could see her smiling through the phone, "He is going to meet you at Bois Restaurant."

"Oh great, now I have to change."

"I'm sure what you have on is fine Angel."

"Carol, okay so how will I know it's him?"

"Okay, I told him you would have your small red scarf wrapped around your wrist."

"How do you know I have a red scarf?"

"I didn't."

I laughed sarcastically. "Oh wow Carol, great guess."

"Angel, stop it"

"I can't. I'm nervous!"

"Okay calm down. He will have on a grey suit with a blue tie."

"Okay"

"Micah will be with your mom right?"

"Right"

"Okay good, call me when you get there. Bye, don't be late, seven o'clock Angel."

"Okay Carol."

"I love you Angel, have fun!"

"Love you too and I'll try."

I turned and faced my young prince, "Okay, Micah how does mommy look?"

Micah held up both thumbs and said, "You look pretty!"

"That's my boy now let's go to Grandma's house."

After I dropped Micah off at my mom's, my heart started to pound. I could hardly hear myself think. Finally, I arrived at the restaurant and called Carol, "Okay, I'm here and I'm on time."

"Very good Angel, you have the scarf on?"

"Yes Carol it's on."

"Okay, now go sit at the bar."

After sitting at the bar for twenty minutes, I was like great he's not coming and I reached for my keys in my purse and suddenly someone tapped me on the shoulder. I turned around and to my surprise it was Michael.

"Angel?" he said.

"Michael?"

We laughed because we were completely shocked, "Oh my goodness...How have you been? And what are you doing here?" I asked.

"Well....I was looking for the woman wearing that red scarf. I didn't know it would be you!"

"Wow! That is crazy Michael. Did Carol and Anthony know that I had already known you?"

"No, they both didn't know and they never said your name."

I could not believe that Michael was the guy that they were talking about. He reached for my hand, "Shall we?" I smiled, "We shall."

He led me to the table where we talked and shared stories. He told me that the reason as to why he had never been married was because of what happened between us. He didn't want to marry anyone else and so he decided to be alone and that the Lord told him don't give up because the woman of his dreams is still out there. I told him that I had finally become a minister and that I had a son and had an amazing journey.

"I see you have forgiven me."

"Oh, Angel, I had to once I saw your face when you turned around."

"Michael I'm sorry."

"Hey, we are not here to talk about the past."

"Yeah you're right." We continued to talk and my heart was filled with so much joy. I couldn't stop smiling.

That night I really had a great time with Michael. I called Carol and told her everything and she was so happy. I had to thank my Father and her for convincing me to go. My life was blossoming and I was so happy. Michael and I would talk every night and go out whenever we could. He even got a chance to meet my son and Micah liked him a lot. I was so happy. But even though I was happy, my spirit began to toss and turn even more on the inside of me.

"Father, why is my spirit restless?"

"Because it's time," he answered.

"Time for what?"

"For you to go back to the church."

"So you are telling me that my Spirit is restless because I'm not in church?"

"Yes Angel, your Spirit needs that worship and fellowship. And in order for us to get you to destiny, you have to be in church."

"I thought everything was all good with me having service in my living room with my baby, I thought that was enough Father. I don't want to go back to my old church, especially with all that I know now and no one will be receptive to me. They haven't in years, they're the same old people with the same old ways and I don't feel like dealing with that."

"Angel you don't go to church for people, you go to church for spiritual growth, to worship, and praise me. It's not about

people. "People will change, yes, but have I changed?"

"Okay Father, where will I go?"

"You will know where to go."

A week after having that conversation with my Father, I decided that since Michael was coming down, I would get some groceries and cook him a nice meal at my place. As Micah and I were at the grocery store, I noticed an older man with gray hair and a walking stick looking at his watch. He then looked up at me and stared at me for a long time. I waved at him and he began to walk my way. "Oh Lord he's crazy," I murmured.

He greeted me, "Hey how are you?"

I smiled, "I'm good, how are you?"

"Oh I'm blessed."

I said to myself, 'okay he's not crazy?'

I see you have a son, "Hi there little guy."

"Hi, my name is Micah," Micah replied.

"Oh like in the bible?"

"Yeah," That's what my mommy said."

"Okay then, looks like your mommy knows the bible very well."

"She does, she reads it to me all the time."

The man smiled, "She does? That's wonderful."

He looked up at me, "God bless you woman of God. That is wonderful what you are doing with your son, teaching him about the Lord."

"That's my job."

Before the old man turned to walk away he leaned towards me, "You're still anointed Angel."

I looked at him, "What?"

"I said you are still Anointed."

"How did you know my name was Angel?"

"Oh, I didn't know, but God knows everything. I'm Pastor Wayne Thomas, pleased to meet you. You are an awesome woman of God, you know that? And God loves you and that little boy so very much that he watches over you two and talks to you both. Tell me, how did you get so much favor with the Lord?"

"I don't understand what you're saying sir, I mean…I know what you are saying, but I don't know why you're saying it."

"Listen Angel read my lips, you-are-still-anointed. Now have a blessed day." He slowly turned around and walked away as I stood there in the middle of the aisle in shock.

While cooking dinner, I guess that Michael could feel that there was something on my mind. He asked me about it and I told him.

Michael laughed. "Oh I see you are still as stubborn as they come."

"Oh come on I'm not stubborn, I wrestle. It's my nature to wrestle."

"Okay Jacob," Michael replied.

"He got blessed, did he not?"

"Angel, there are a lot of people that need to hear what God has to say through you. Your Father is only trying to help and use you at the same time."

"I know but I don't want to go back to my old church, you know."

"Hey, you don't have to. Look at this as a fresh start. You can come to my church for a while."

"I am not driving three hours to church every morning no way!"

"Okay, yeah you're right. I can't have you and Micah getting up early in the morning."

"Yeah I know."

"Well didn't the man say he was a Pastor?"

"Yes he did."

'Well go to his church."

"You know what Michael, I think I may just do that, maybe I could Google him."

Michael shook his head, "Angel you Google everything."

After Micah went to bed and Michael left for the night, I Googled Pastor Thomas to see where he preached. The search results all pointed towards "Saving Lives Outreach Ministry." I wrote down the address and decided to go that following Sunday.

As Micah and I got out of the car, there were so many people lined up to get into this small church. Micah looked at me, "Mommy we're late."

"No we're not baby it's just too many people for this small church." We finally walked through the doors as Pastor Thomas began to minister. It was so powerful and half of the church was laid on the floor. He beckoned for me to come to the front.

Micah and I walked through the aisles. He said to one of his ushers, "Hold the baby's hand."

I saw a lady come and grab Micah's hand. Pastor Thomas looked at me as I looked at Micah with concern, "He's alright Angel. Now you lift up your hands." He pointed to me, "For every door that was shut, God said that that's how many doors will be opened plus more. You have been chosen to do something great for the Lord. The very same people that counted you out will want you to come speak for them later. He will make your enemies your foot stool. He's been with you Angel, through it all, you are blessed, what is the date?!" He shouted out to the congregation.

Someone shouted, "The eleventh of June!"

He pointed at me "This time next year Angel, God said your name will be changed and so will your life!"

I shouted, "Yes, Lord Jesus!" and finally after so many years, I cried.

"There it is," Pastor Thomas said, "You haven't cried in year's baby. Let it out and you needed this moment right here. I'm not here to hurt you and we will not judge you, but I will make sure that you get to where God needs you to be."

I looked at Micah and he started to cry and he ran and gave me a hug, "I love you mommy." I felt so much better after service.

One of the Ushers came and told me that Pastor Thomas wanted to speak with me before I left. I quickly went to the back where Pastor Thomas was. "Angel, I knew you would come. You're blessed girl. Come sit down, it's okay."

I sat down and Micah sat in my lap. Pastor Thomas and I talked until the church was empty and after his wife came in and said that they had to get going. She turned towards me, "You must be Angel?"

"Yes ma'am I am."

She hugged me tight, "God bless you Angel. It is so wonderful to be in your presence!"

"Thank you ma'am, same to you"

She looked at Pastor Thomas. He smiled and we all said a prayer and left.

That following Friday, Michael asked me if he could take Micah on a "Man's day out" and I agreed because I really needed some time to think about whether or not I was going to really go back to the church. I had to talk to my Father.

"Father, I have been through so much in my life and you have been there every step of the way. I have seen how cruel people can be, especially church folk and it's like I let you down every time I get involved with church. For the first time I don't feel like I have let you down because I have had church in my home instead of going out. I know that being in church and fellowship is important, but I don't feel like dealing with that anymore. I know that we go to church to worship and praise you, and for the first time in a long time, I actually went to a church and I felt amazing afterwards, but now I don't know if I can do this again."

"Angel, are you afraid of falling again?" the Lord asked.

"Yes Father, but that's not just all."

"Angel, life is filled with experiences, and yes some of those experiences may cause you to be hurt. But it is not to hurt you or destroy you, but it is for you to take what has hurt you and learn from it and grow from it. It makes you stronger. It makes you wiser. You can't beat yourself up nor isolate yourself because of other people's mishaps or lack of understanding."

(Sigh) "Okay, I'll go Father, for you I'll go back to church under one condition."

"What's that?"

"Only if you Father enlarge my territory"

"As long as you are faithful Angel, that request shall always be granted"

After speaking with my Father, our Lord our Savior, I went back to the church. Pastor Thomas was thrilled that after being there for over eight months, I finally decided to join his ministry. After serving under Pastor Thomas and sitting under his teachings and absorbing every piece of information, I felt myself growing. My confidence came back, not only was God my father my protector, my healer, my provider, my council, but I realized that he sent Pastor Thomas and his wife whom he had raised up under his wing to be great mentors. And that the job of mentors was just like His, not to be over Him, but to help make sure that His sons and daughters have those types of leaders that will help them to learn, grown, and stay on the right track. I cherished every time spent and every moment. I was finally patient and I felt restored. The ministry that God had placed on my life began to grow again and for the first time, I actually knew who I was in the Lord. I knew my purpose and because I knew my purpose, I was able to stand out boldly and not hold back. I could pour into others and mentor others. After serving under Pastor Thomas for two years, the congregation was in a new sanctuary and Michael had asked for my hand in marriage. I said yes and the following year, I was married to the man that I thought I would never see again: my college sweetheart, Michael Smoother.

"Well Angel," Pastor Thomas said while we were standing in his brand new office, "It has definitely been an amazing journey."

"Yes it has Pastor!"

"You are ready daughter. I have seen you grow and have married you off. When you walk out of those doors, every step you take from then are the steps of destiny. But remember that even on your best day, you are still nothing compared to God."

"Thank you Pastor Thomas. Thank you for seeing who God said that I was and thank you for not turning you back on me and not giving up on me. I thank God for you and your wife, for this ministry, and all that you all have done for me and my son, we thank you so much." I then hugged Pastor Thomas and walked out of his office.

A month later, I had to preach at this annual revival at New Way Church International. It felt so good to be back in that element that God had created for us ministers. The people were praising God and it had now come time for healing and deliverance at the altar. Before I started to pray, I looked into the crowd of people, and saw a lady wearing a purple dress standing in the back. I suddenly heard the Lord say, **"Walk closer."** The closer I came towards her; I realized that it was Remi. I ran the rest of the way to her and embraced her with a hug as tears began to roll from our eyes. Even though service was going forth, I just had to do what I felt in my heart. I looked at her and she looked so frail. She was smaller than I had remembered and when I looked her in her eyes and told her I loved her, she broke down in tears. I grabbed her hand as we walked towards the altar, and began to pray over her and everyone else that wanted prayer. After the service, Remi stuck around to catch up with me.

"Oh my God, Angel, it has been a very, very long time."

"Yes it has, how are you Remi?"

Remi looked down and cleared her throat, "I have breast cancer Angel."

"No you don't Remi. This day, you Remi, you are healed by the blood of Jesus."

"Oh I deserve it Angel, for how I treated you and others."

"Remi no one deserves to be sick, and besides why say that you are; or what you deserve when you are neither the author nor the finisher of your life?"

"How can you be so nice to me after all I said to you Angel? How can you forgive me? I said all of those hurtful things to you and now look at you; you have more than I will ever have."

"Remi, you have just as much as I do and that is Jesus Christ. It's not about having more than the other; it's about having Him who is everything."

"Angel I'm sorry and I have a question?"

"What's that?"

"How do I get to know the God you serve?"

I looked at Remi with a smile, "Girl I thought you would never ask."

After that day, my friendship with Remi was restored. It was a tough fight for her, but she was truly healed from breast cancer. I thought about Ava, but before I could search for her, she called.

"Angel!" She screamed on the phone.

"Ava! How did you find me?"

"Well let's just say I have my ways."

"How in the world have you been Ava?" She told me about how after she had finished school, she stayed in the area and settled down there and had a son and I told her how I was married and had a son as well. She was so excited. I then asked her, her sons name and she said that it was Milton. I told her that my son's name was Micah. We laughed and said that it's something about the names that start with the letter M.

We couldn't really talk that long because I had a beep coming in from a number that I did not recognize but I knew I had to answer it so I told her I would call her back. I answered the beep…

"Hello is this Angel?" the man asked.

"Speaking."

"Hi, Angel!"

"Hi, may I ask who am I speaking with?"

The man hesitated for a while, "It's your Father."

My heart sunk into my chest as I began to take deep breaths and said softly, "Pastor Peers?"

"Yes Angel, Pastor Peers."

"Does your wife know that you are calling me?"

"Yes she knows."

Tears fell from my eyes, "And she knows I'm your daughter?"

"Yes Angel she knows. I see your mother finally told you huh?"

"Yes, she did many years ago. Why couldn't you say anything?"

"I'm sorry Angel. I'm so sorry. I should have said something. I should have told you. I should have told my wife. I should have done things a lot different, but you know what, I am doing things different now and I want my daughter in my life. You are the only child that I have in this world. I have been a father figure to every child in my congregation and across the world and I have not been anything close to that to you. Even when you came under my ministry, I yet and still neglected you and practically left you. But not anymore, please forgive me Angel I'm so sorry."

I looked up as water flowed from my eyes. "Pastor Peers, for years I believed that another man was my Father until he and my mother told me otherwise. I always asked myself how someone could know that there is someone that they helped conceive living amongst them and they have no heart or can't muster up a conversation with them or even acknowledge that they even existed. What you and my mom did cursed me. I too had a child by a man of your status who left me to raise a son alone and I never went into detail with my mom about you guys' situation but I always prayed that you didn't treat her the way that man treated me. She never loved again because she was manipulated and scorned. And that curse has been broken. It will not reoccur into Micah's life or any of his children. I forgive you, I already did. And I can tell you this, you weren't there but there was someone who made sure that I wasn't a woman to be scorned because of her Dad's mistakes. And that man is Jesus. You could not imagine how much this man loves me and even on your best day of mentoring and being a spiritual Father to many could not and would never compare to all he has done and been to me! So no you will not have the title Father to me because He has proved himself worthy of that title even though He did not have to. You may not be my Father, but you are my Dad and I forgive you and I love you."

"Wow Angel, I know that I will never compare. Thank you and I'll respect that. Angel, can I be your Dad? And if so, when can I start?"

"Pastor Peers you started when you called."

After having a long conversation with my dad, it was refreshing to finally hear him call me his daughter after so many years. We became closer and restored our relationship. His wife wasn't really too happy about it, but after a while, she finally came around and accepted me into their family. I am sure it wasn't an easy pill to swallow, but she did it and that said a lot about her and what she stood for. It was the right thing to do. A few weeks later, I received a phone call from my dad saying that he wanted me to preach at this event for him because he was unable to do so and I agreed. While preparing for an event in the state of Georgia, I asked Remi and Ava to join me on that night. Ava and I still didn't get a chance to talk much so I told her after the service, we all would sit down and catch up and she agreed.

The night had finally arrived and I did not expect what I saw for this program. The building was as big as a stadium and there were cars parked as far as I could see. I finally walked inside the building and a lady met me with a microphone attached to her ear and said, "Follow me." She rushed me to the back office. I sat down in the room with my husband Michael and my son Micah.

My husband looked at me and smiled, "Baby did you know you were going to be preaching here?"

"No, I just agreed to do this for my Dad. I didn't know it was going to be this many people."

Michael rubbed his hands together, "Okay let's pray."

As soon as he finished the prayer, my Dad came into the office. I stood up, "What are you doing here?"

"Baby girl, it's your time, to share your story with the world. Now I know that I have not been there for you. I thank God for having another chance to be your Dad. Now it's time for you to tell the world about your Father, Our Lord and Savior Jesus Christ. I came because I would not miss this moment for nothing in the world. It is your time to share with us the "Heart of God."

The room became silent. I could hear the service begin and the uproar of 40,000 people. I asked my dad and my husband, and son to leave the room for just a minute.

I slowly got down on my knees, "Father I thank you, and I love you so much, you are the reason I live; you are the reason I breathe. My love for you goes beyond the skies and runs deeper than any ocean. Thank you for raising me up for such a time as this. Thank you for teaching me your love at the tender age of eleven and thank you for molding me. You never said it would be easy and after every bad choice and every wrong decision, you were there to catch me every time you saw that I had begun to fall. You taught me how to love. You taught me that love was relationship, patience, unconditional love, endurance, grace, compassion, and joy. You taught me love. You taught me how to love even when I didn't want too. You taught me how to live even though I couldn't see the blessing. You taught me how to press towards the mark for the prize of the higher calling of God in Christ Jesus. No one will ever have your heart. For we even must ask you dear Lord to create in us a clean heart. If an individual had the heart that you have, they would not be able to contain it in their mortal bodies. Lord! I kneel to show my humility before you, for I am your servant; I will greatly serve you Lord as your ambassador. I now know that I am the Daughter of the King because I know the Heart of God."

I was interrupted by a knock at the door, and I suddenly heard my phone vibrate. I said that I would answer my phone after service. My husband entered the room, "Baby it's time."

I looked up at my Father and whispered, "Even on my best day, I am still nothing compared to you. You go first and I'll follow."

I looked at my husband, exhaled, and slowly counted to five. I heard my Father whisper in my ear, **"Let's go."**

"From start to finish."

"From the beginning to the end."

I walked out onto that platform and my Father used me to the max and service was wonderful. After service, I had over two hundred phone calls on my cell. However, I wasn't impressed with no one but my Father.

My husband looked at me and said, "You're not going to respond."

"I'll respond tomorrow honey. Today, let's just enjoy what God has blessed."

I decided to have dinner with Remi, Ava, my husband, my mom, my dad and his wife. I was excited to finally introduce my family to my friends and while waiting for Ava and Remi at the restaurant, I heard my phone ring again. I also noticed that, that particular number had called me more than any of the others, so I decided to call back just to see if something was wrong. I asked to be excused for a moment and answered, "Hello?"

"Yes, is this Angel?" a woman said.

"Yes, this is she, how may I help you?"

"I'm calling because I am Pastor Strong's assistant and I had to notify you because he is terribly ill and is asking to see his son."

I hesitated, "Okay, umm, can I call this number back?"

"Sure but the doctor said immediately because there isn't much time."

"Okay I will get back to you shortly."

I went back inside the restaurant and I didn't want to talk about the phone call so I said, "Who's ready to eat?"

Michael asked to be excused to go to the restroom. Finally after I sat down, Remi and Ava and her son walked in. I got up to greet them both and introduced everyone, "My husband had to go to the restroom, but he should be back in a second."

Everyone was smiling and talking and then Michael started walking towards the table. I saw Ava's eyes get bigger, "Ava! I forgot to tell you I married Michael. I never mentioned my husband's name surprise!"

Ava began to frown. "Am I missing something?" I asked. Michael just stood like a statue. "Okay?" I pressed.

Ava looked at me sadly, "I am surprised Angel."

"Great!"

"No Angel it's not great. I'm surprised because I haven't seen Michael in years and do you want to know why?"

I looked at Michael and then looked at Ava, "Why?"

Tears slowly rolled from her eyes as she looked at me and said, "Because Michael is Milton's dad."

Thank You

I hope that you enjoyed the story. At this time I would like to say thank you to the people that was a blessing on helping me put together such a phenomenal piece of Art. I would like to thank:

Our Lord and Savior Jesus Christ

Lew Lampkin

Joshua McMillan

Tiresia McMillan

Pastor Orlando Richmond

And to each and every one of you who purchased a copy God bless you and I love you.

Made in the USA
Columbia, SC
26 November 2023